Rorschach Audio
Art & Illusion for Sound

Joe Banks

Rorschach Audio – Art and Illusion for Sound
Copyright © Joe Banks 2012

Joe Banks has asserted his moral right to be identified as the author of this work in accordance with the Copyright, Designs and Patents Act, 1988. All rights reserved. No part of this publication may be reproduced in any form or by any means without the written permission of the publishers. A CIP catalogue record for this book is available from the British Library.

ISBN 978-1-907222-20-7

Production by Strange Attractor Press
BM SAP, London WC1N 3XX, UK
www.strangeattractor.co.uk

Printed in the UK

Contents

Introduction	vii
Art and Illusion for Sound	9
Burning an Illusion	70
L'Amour / La Mort	114
Let Him Have It, Chris!	150

Introduction

"It is the story of the signaller who misheard the urgent message '*Send reinforcements, am going to advance*' as '*Send three and four pence, am going to a dance*'."
– EH Gombrich *Some Axioms, Musings & Hints on Hearing*

Rorschach Audio - Art and Illusion for Sound is the most recent, and by far the most comprehensive, in an ongoing series of publications which have been continually produced since 1999. The *Rorschach Audio* project began as an attempt to analyse claims made by self-styled Electronic Voice Phenomena researchers, about the allegedly supernatural origin of voice recordings which EVP researchers believe constitute objective and scientific proof of the existence of the afterlife, but which instead this project categorises as illusions of sound. As the great physicist, debunker of fraudulent Spiritualism and in fact devout Christian Michael Faraday said of his classic lecture *The Chemical History of the Candle*, it is hoped that a critical study of these phenomena will prove valuable, not least because it provides many opportunities to "an open door by which you can enter into the study of natural philosophy"*. In that sense this project not only explains EVP as psychoacoustic (rather than ghostly) phenomena, but also explores relevant aspects of psychology of perception, scientific method and philosophy of science etc.

While the central metaphor proposed by this project draws an analogy between the interpretation of ambiguous voice recordings and illusory interpretations of the famous Rorschach ink-blot tests, a central text of this critique is an internal memorandum circulated within the BBC Monitoring Service during WW2, and *Rorschach Audio* is unique in emphasising the influence that wartime intelligence work with *sound* had on one of the most important works of *visual* arts theory ever published – *Art and Illusion* by EH Gombrich. Following that lead, this volume explores many related subjects, in a collection of chapters which have been developed from earlier, originally separate and self-contained articles and lectures etc. In terms of narrative these chapters are therefore thematic rather than chronologically sequential, and inevitably these chapters overlap occasionally as a result. The first chapter focusses on EVP, psychoacoustics and relationships between science and technology; the second on the social history of EVP, particularly on links between EVP and Spiritualism; the third explores relationships between illusions, mishearing and artistic creativity; the fourth focusses on relationships between auditory and visual illusions; and in all cases it is hoped these chapters will prove as entertaining and informative to read as they were to write.

Acknowledgements to the many friends, colleagues, individuals and institutions who have contributed to this project are listed on a chapter-by-chapter basis, however the acknowledgement that applies most to the entire project is to The Arts and Humanities Research Council, which supported this publication, and which, for the last five years, supported the *Rorschach Audio* project itself.

Joe Banks, The University of Westminster, April 2012

* Colin Russell *Michael Faraday - Physics and Faith* Oxford University Press, 2000, p.76

Chapter 1
Art and Illusion for Sound

"Sometimes we see a cloud that's dragonish;
A vapour sometime like a bear or lion,
A tower'd citadel, a pendant rock,
A forked mountain, or blue promontory
With trees upon't, that nod unto the world,
And mock our eyes with air."
– Shakespeare *Antony & Cleopatra*

"Bull's eyes and targets,
Say the bells of St Margaret's.
Brickbats and tiles,
Say the bells of St Giles.
Oranges and lemons,
Say the bells of St Clement's.
Two sticks and an apple,
Say the bells at Whitechapel,
Old Father Baldpate,
Say the slow bells at Aldgate.
You owe me ten shillings,
Say the bells at St Helen's.
When will you pay me?
Say the bells at Old Bailey.
When I grow rich,
Say the bells at Fleet Ditch."
– Anonymous *London Bells*

The title of this book – *Rorschach Audio* – is taken from an article written for the sleevenotes of a compact disc called *The Ghost Orchid*, subtitled *An Introduction to Electronic Voice Phenomena* [1], published in 1999. For those who may be unaware, Electronic Voice Phenomena are a class of allegedly "mysterious" vocal recordings, and while several explanations have been offered to explain how they originate, the overwhelming majority of those who research the subject of EVP believe that the recordings they have made constitute physical evidence of contact with the afterlife (and *The Ghost Orchid* CD documented a number of the better-known examples of such recordings). In other words EVP researchers mostly believe that, using radios, microphones and tape recorders (and more recently also computers, video cameras and televisions etc), it is possible to literally record the voices (and images) of phantoms, spirits, poltergeists, ghosts. The original *Rorschach Audio* sleevenotes offered a critique of those beliefs, and the version of *Rorschach Audio* published here is the product of an extended process of research and revision which has taken place more-or-less continually ever since.

The great scientists Edison and Marconi both believed in the possibility that radio technology might enable contact with the afterlife – an idea that sits well in the context of Victorian enthusiasm for various forms of Spiritualism; however the EVP movement proper began in 1957 when Friedrich Jürgenson, an artist who painted portraits of Pope Pius XII, found human voices intruding on recordings he had made of his own voice and then, in 1959, of birdsong. Convinced that these recordings represented communications from alien lifeforms and, for instance, his deceased mother, Jürgenson temporarily abandoned his artistic career to concentrate on these experiments and to publicise his findings. In 1960 he started recording similar voices with radio equipment, then published the books *Rösterna Från Rymden* (The Voices from Space) [2] in 1964, *Sprechfunk Mit Verstorbenen* (Voice Transmissions With The Deceased) in 1967 [3], and *Radio och Mikrofonkontakt med de Döda* (Radio and Microphone Contact with the Dead) [4] in 1968. From 1968 onwards Jürgenson cemented an increasingly a close relationship with the Vatican, making a number of documentary films about religious themes, and executing portrait commissions for Pope Paul VI [5]. Jürgenson's publications, and particularly the idea that he had amassed evidence proving the existence of the afterlife, attracted considerable attention, including that of Konstantin Raudive, who took up the cause of EVP research, allegedly making tens of thousands of recordings.

Through the publication of his book *Breakthrough* in 1971 [6] Raudive became the leading light in an international circle of EVP enthusiasts, and today the movement that Jürgenson and Raudive effectively founded has evolved into a widespread activity of such complexity that a truly comprehensive survey would be beyond the scope of this present chapter. So, while the subject of EVP history, and particularly the story of the EVP movement's historic relationship with Spiritualism, will be explored in more detail in a later chapter, the purpose of this first chapter is to cut straight to the chase, in addressing the major, salient issues which recur throughout EVP research and which in fact underpin the entire belief system. This chapter will argue that EVP represents a classic example of the supposedly strange phenomenon for which there is the proverbial "perfectly rational explanation", but will argue that a critical discussion of EVP can nonetheless still be a rewarding and valuable exercise, even for those who never did believe in the supernatural "reality" of EVP recordings. This is because, having studied the subject in some detail, I came to realise that EVP beliefs have their origin in psychological processes which influence the entire process of human perception, and whose study is therefore interesting and important, for the simple reason that these processes are shared by everyone. Similarly, understanding how the evidence provided by EVP experiments has become the basis of a complex, often entrenched belief system is of genuine anthropological interest, not least because the process entails the use of electronic technology to help construct, rationalise and validate a fundamentally anti-scientific belief system.

The material presented will also be used to support a second hypothesis – that an understanding of the processes involved in EVP may also contribute to theories of art criticism, both in general terms and with particular reference to music and especially to contemporary sound art. It has to be said that the ideas on which these hypotheses are based are not innovative, that they are already embedded in mainstream critical theory, and that they trace direct descent from an individual generally recognised as the most important figure in the history of Western art. What is most surprising about these ideas is not their existence as such, but the extent to which they, like sound art in general, have previously been ignored. Ideas which were primarily developed to explain certain aspects of visual perception and to enhance the appreciation of visual art also have great relevance to issues of acoustic perception, although this aspect of their interpretation seems to have received relatively scant attention. While a body of anecdotal and experimental evidence does exist connecting visual art theories to ideas about acoustic perception, to the best of my knowledge this material is still highly dispersed (even when updating this research in 2012) and has not previously been either adequately grouped together or seriously applied to issues such as assessing EVP or understanding sound art.

Speaking personally, my first exposure to examples of Electronic Voice Phenomena recordings was when, as a teenager, one of the other kids at school brought in a flexidisc of voices recorded by Konstantin Raudive. The flexidisc turned-up in 1982, having been given away free on the cover of *The Unexplained* magazine [7], however the recordings it featured had originally been released a decade earlier as a 7-inch vinyl record, published to accompany Raudive's book *Breakthrough*. These recordings are now reproduced in full, among many others, on *The Ghost Orchid* CD. In contrast to the chore of trawling through the thousands of transcribed voice recordings which are detailed in Raudive's book, on the vinyl records, these examples have been edited down to a frankly unique work of audio propaganda. The style of these recordings is typical of EVP – after introducing the general subject, narrators Nadia Fowler and Michael Smythe introduce a series of voice recordings which manifest as brief bursts of extremely distorted sounds and voices, accompanied by very high levels of radio interference, and by what appears to be motor noise picked from the recording apparatus by a microphone. The examples are repeated several times and the general ambience of the recordings is menacing.

So, for instance, the narration on the *Breakthrough* record states that Raudive called out to his deceased friend Margarete Petrautzki, asking "how she felt in the beyond?" The ghost replied "bedenke, ich bin", which the narration translates as "German – imagine, I am". The ghost also says the name of her former employer "Zenta", answers "Kostya ja" – "Kostya yes" (referring to Raudive's nickname), and, in one of the least convincing examples, is alleged to have said "Raudiv", but in fact the relevant extract sounds more like just "Row". The record features other ghosts, including the Spanish philosopher José Ortega Y Gasset, British wartime Prime Minister Winston Churchill, and the Futurist poet Vladimir Mayakovsky, who responds to a statement about "how difficult it is to convince people of the reality of the voice phenomenon" by telling the experimenter "Konstantin plui", which is translated as "Russian – Konstantin spit on it". Observing audience responses to these recordings at *Rorschach Audio* lecture-demonstrations seems to confirm, at least anecdotally, that my own reaction to this material had been fairly typical. Many of the voice samples, and particularly the meanings that the narrators attributed to them, come across as genuinely risible. During these lectures, the smiles occasionally stop however when audiences hear examples that do come across as, if not convincing, then at least unnerving, and, although the record's overall ambience may have as much to do with Nadia Fowler's striking narrative style as it has to do with the content of Raudive's recordings, this record packs an undeniable punch in terms of creating a truly vivid atmosphere. Like some faintly sinister antique that one might rescue from a dilapidated junk shop, if nothing else these recordings rank as a world-class phonological curio, because, as a dramatic performance, the record conjures a definite sense of being present during what amounts to an actual séance, and it is probably for this reason that the *Breakthrough* record has acquired the status of a minor legend, particularly among electronic musicians and sound artists.

Spooky theatrics notwithstanding, even as a teenager my initial reaction to hearing the *Breakthrough* record was one of sheer disbelief, since in addition to instinctive scepticism about any claims about the existence of the supernatural, outright forgery of such material would be absolute child's play. It seemed amazing that, in assuming shared faith in the alleged origin of these recordings, the record's publishers had the confidence to expect such a degree of gullibility on behalf of their audience. It seemed obvious that the most primitive tape recording and overdubbing techniques could easily produce recordings of this nature – not least because the more basic the technology used, the lower the signal-to-noise ratio would be, and the more the finished product would resonate with an aura of menacing low-fidelity mystique, which can even help impart a subjective impression of authenticity to such material. Put simply, one paradox of EVP is that if the voices recorded were of similar quality to normal high-fidelity studio recordings of speech, then nobody would believe in them for a minute. If someone came to you claiming that they possessed a recording dictated after death by one of your own close relatives, and they then played a high-quality recording of a stranger speaking in a normal voice, it's reasonable to assume that most people would be not so much convinced as instead quite deeply insulted; and it is a strange fact that it is because of, rather than despite, the very low sound quality of most EVP recordings, that at least some listeners are seduced into suspending disbelief. A better production would, ironically, be less convincing.

Having openly confessed that my initial attitude to EVP was instinctively negative however, it may be another paradox of these phenomena that, unlike many "scientific" responses to paranormal research, the discourse presented in *Rorschach Audio* is categorically not based on dismissing the claims of EVP researchers out of hand. As we will see, the hypotheses developed in *Rorschach Audio* are instead predicated on taking many of the researchers' claims at face value, as this book will argue that some EVP researchers, although misguided, may well have genuine motives, and that many of the signals they have recorded are not consciously faked after all, but that these sounds instead represent commonplace and materially real physical phenomena, albeit phenomena whose origin and nature the EVP researchers have fundamentally misunderstood.

The suggestion that EVP could be described as "real" phenomena, and that explanations do exist to account for how they arise is drawn from a number of sources. The neurologist Oliver Sacks discusses the subject of acoustic projection in his book *Seeing Voices* [8], quoting descriptions of the "eye music" and "phantasmal voices" experienced by the South African poet David Wright (1920-1994), as described in Wright's autobiographical book *Deafness* [9]. David Wright sustained profound hearing damage at the age of seven after contracting scarlet fever, at the age of 13 he emigrated, and was then educated at The Northampton School for the Deaf in England. Partly because deafness stuck at an age after which he had already acquired spoken language, Wright later found himself able to experience reconstructed sound images projected by his mind into his perceived environment as an extension of visual information. So, for example, lip-reading triggered actual voices inside David Wright's head, despite the fact that no environmental cues were being provided by his ears. The projecting effect was so strong in fact that David Wright even reported perceiving ghost sounds conjured in his mind by the motion of trees in wind.

Wright explained that "my deafness was made more difficult to perceive because from the very first my eyes had unconsciously begun to translate motion into sound.

My mother spent most of the day beside me and I understood everything she said. Why not? Without knowing it I had been reading her mouth all my life. When she spoke I seemed to hear her voice. It was an illusion which persisted even after I knew it was an illusion. My father, my cousin, everyone I had known retained phantasmal voices. That they were imaginary, the projections of habit and memory, did not come home to me until I had left the hospital. One day I was talking with my cousin and he, in a moment of inspiration, covered his mouth with his hand as he spoke. Silence!" Oliver Sacks also describes similar examples involving anosmia – the loss of the sense of smell, blindness and the "ghost" or "phantom" limbs experienced by some amputees – and the neurologist Vilayanur Ramachandran has achieved extraordinary results in "severing" such ghost limbs with... mirrors [10].

Astonishing and unusual as they may be, Wright's faculties were however simply highly-developed versions of a capacity for projection that this discourse will argue not only manifests in all senses in all people, able-bodied or otherwise, but which paradoxically underpins the entire process of normal perception. One illustration of this is a phenomenon referred to as The McGurk Effect, which suggests that techniques applied by skilled lip-readers are also important for normal day-to-day speech perception. The McGurk Effect takes its name from the now famous experiment in which psychologists Harry McGurk and John MacDonald showed a film of a speaking face to volunteers [11]. The face and lips made movements that were correct for its original soundtrack, which had consisted of the speaker repeating the sound "ga" over and over again. However, in the version of the film that was presented to the experimental test-subjects, the sound "ga" was removed and replaced with "ba", lip-synched into the correct position in the video soundtrack. What listeners perceived was (bizarrely) neither "ga" nor "ba" – instead they heard "da", which is phonetically between "ga" and "ba".

What seems to be happening with The McGurk Effect is that the brain senses the film's soundtrack through the normal physical apparatus of hearing, but, before interpreting and perceiving that sense-data, the mind then projects meaning onto it, with that meaning being partly based on information that has been derived from non-audio sources – in this case, from vision. Such processes are not at all unusual. If we did not for instance project meaning onto sounds in accordance with information derived from other sources (such as, to take another example, memory) then all voices would be perceived as though they were being spoken in foreign languages, because it is our *recollection* of our own language that enables us to perceive those sounds correctly. It is a statement so obvious as to be almost trite, that the only reason we understand our native tongue is because we have learned the words from which it is comprised, so it is our memories of those words which allow us to retrieve and to project meanings onto sounds that would otherwise be perceived as foreign. With The McGurk Effect, an equivalent process takes place in terms of the interaction between hearing and vision, with the sounds being modified by the brain's memory of what should have emerged from the lip movements that had just been seen.

From the perspective of both developmental psychology and evolutionary biology, the strength of the connection between lip-reading and hearing suggested by The McGurk Effect makes perfect sense, because one of the earliest, most primal and profound experiences that humans share is the process of acquiring spoken language from watching the lips and eyes of their parents. In this sense, the relationship between lip-reading and hearing is not surprising at all, but is instead one of the most fundamental and deeply encoded aspects of human speech perception. A great deal has been said in art circles about the fascinating subject of synaesthesia – the experience whereby, in rare individuals, perceptions spill-over and induce abilities to see sounds, taste colours etc, and, although subtle, The McGurk Effect is arguably related to synaesthesia, although it can be experienced by virtually everyone. The original McGurk Effect video has been posted on the video sharing website YouTube, and readers are strongly encouraged to try this experience for themselves. In marked contrast to the ambience of the *Breakthrough* recordings, the atmosphere of this video is somewhat "dry" to say the least, but the effect becomes altogether more impressive when listeners realise that the sound they hear actually changes according to whether their eyes are open or closed [12].

A more commonplace and familiar example, which will on some level be well-known to almost everybody (irrespective of what they actually drink at social gatherings) is the famous Cocktail Party Effect, which was identified by the American psychologist Colin Cherry in 1953 [13]. It is certainly pertinent to the broader themes of *Rorschach Audio* that a good deal of Colin Cherry's work on this phenomenon arose from trying to resolve difficulties that air traffic controllers experience in extracting meaning from the "babel" of radio chatter produced by civilian and military pilots, and this phenomenon is as relevant to clear communication within battle management systems as it is to genteel social chit-chat. Readers can demonstrate the Cocktail Party Effect for themselves by recording ambient sounds of conversational chatter that are typical of most busy social environments – listening to such recordings, it is often hard (if not impossible) to extract and to accurately follow individual conversations within the cacophony, but there wouldn't be much point in socialising at all if people couldn't successfully follow live conversations in-situ. Barry Arons of The MIT Media Lab points out the paradox that "from a listener's point of view..." the necessary process of extraction "...is intuitive and simple", while "from a psychological or physiological perspective there is a vast and complex array of evidence that has to be pieced together to explain the effect" [14]. Among other factors, one of the main reasons that we are able to extract individual conversations from ambient social chatter is because, unlike someone listening to a tape, live listeners are able to lip-read the faces of those to whom they are directly speaking, and in such cases, as with The McGurk Effect, visual information heavily modifies the interpretations that are projected onto the sounds heard by the mind.

Although in everyday language the terms "sensing" and "perceiving" can be used for most purposes to mean more-or-less the same thing, in the context of this discussion it can be helpful to refine a distinction between sensation and perception. In more exact usage the word "sensation" refers to the process whereby sense-organs (such as the ears, eyes, nose, tongue etc) mechanically collect raw and uninterpreted sense-data from the individual's environment, while the word "perception" refers to the process by which the mind projects meanings onto that sense-data, and projection phenomena illustrate the apparent paradox that even superficially physical aspects of hearing are also partly psychological (in fact this paradox is only really linguistic, as in the underlying process there is no fundamental paradox at all, since all psychological processes are ultimately physical).

Research quoted earlier referred to a "babel" of radio communications, and among wartime experiences related in his autobiographical novel the *The Periodic Table* [15], the anti-fascist partisan and industrial chemist Primo Levi recalled a laboratory test apparatus called a heterodyne which, under certain conditions, functioned as a radio receiver. Primo Levi described an "intricate universe of mysterious messages, morse tickings, modulated hisses, deformed, mangled human voices which pronounced sentences in incomprehensible languages or in code… messages of death… the radiophonic Babel of war", and it is perhaps not surprising that studies of sounds of wartime radio also provide useful clues which help resolve the enigma of EVP. Olive Renier and Vladimir Rubinstein's book *Assigned to Listen* [16] describes the "ether war" fought by The BBC Monitoring Service, which scanned WW2's "remorseless sea of noises" for the broken voices, coded messages, news, propaganda, disinformation and entertainment broadcasts that fought for bandwidth with the incessant vagaries of ionospheric propagation and the turbulence of electrical and magnetic storms.

Although the premises itself now operates as a hotel and as a conference centre, The BBC Monitoring Service still operates from the grounds of Wood Norton Hall – memorably described as "Colditz on Avon" [17] – a country house located in the "electrically quiet" location of Caversham, Worcestershire [18]. In terms of physical atmosphere, travel writer Simon Calder reports that Wood Norton Hall was originally owned by French aristocrat the Duc d'Aumale, son of King Louis-Phillipe, and that this "marvelously pretentious baronial pile" is listed as a Grade 2 building "presumably for its comedy value", as "the unfulfilled heirs to the French throne set about avenging their dispossession by imposing their regal emblem upon every surface". Presumably their emblem is not used to decorate the Bredon Wing – the massive underground bunker that was built at BBC Caversham for use as an emergency broadcast centre in the event of a nuclear war [19].

The explosion of radio communications that occurred before and during WW2 created an urgent requirement for an institution capable of "systematic listening" [20] –

"The Ears of Britain", as The BBC Monitoring Service is sometimes known, is funded by The Foreign Office, The Cabinet Office, The BBC World Service and The Ministry of Defence. The service employs many highly-skilled foreign language translators, and during WW2 these researchers were a "polyglot team" [21] of intellectuals, linguists and even poets, many of whom had escaped Europe as refugees from Nazism (similarly, today, many employees are asylum seekers who have also escaped dictatorships and repressive regimes). During WW2 the service's Monitoring Department passed transcripts of intercepted radio broadcasts to their Editorial Department, who compiled printed intelligence reports known as "Digests", which were reported up to clients including Downing Street, government ministries and military intelligence. The Editorial Department tended to recruit from radio producers and journalists – "a select group of troglodytes" – one of whom was in fact my grandad (who did, for many years, really live in a cave).

Magnetic tape recorders were not introduced until the end of the WW2, so the method employed by the BBC Monitors was to record what were often already weak, indistinct and sometimes highly garbled radio signals onto Ediphone "transcribers" – primitive dictation machines whose wax cylinders could be re-used, after transcription, by shaving down and re-smoothing the surface of the cylinder. Renier and Rubinstein recalled that "the cylinders were not always shaved very cleanly, and occasionally part-passages and odd words or sounds from previous recordings could be heard... this intermingling could cause confusion and was fraught with danger". Not surprisingly such factors conspired to degrade the quality of discernible intelligence to the point at which the monitors often struggled to make sense of their recordings (inviting comparisons with the kinds of problems encountered by, for instance, photo reconnaissance analysts and restorers of antique paintings). To return to the point however, the necessity for methodically re-analysing noisy voice recordings over and over to detect faint traces of intelligence is virtually identical to some EVP research techniques, but *Assigned to Listen* makes no mention of any monitor ever ascribing any signal to ghosts.

In order to assist his colleagues in their work, BBC Monitoring Supervisor Ernst Gombrich circulated a collection of listening tips in an internal memorandum entitled "Some Axioms, Musings and Hints on Hearing" from which *Assigned to Listen* quotes at length. Ernst Gombrich stated that "the mechanism of projection plays a major part in hearing". While stressing that "this crucial fact of Gestalt psychology is not easy to explain in words", Gombrich described acoustic projection as "the mechanism by which we read familiar shapes into clouds, or melodies into the monotonous rattle of a train... in a similar way we can read speech into a medley of noises". In fact, three decades later, the American psychologist Robert Remez created just such a medley of noises when he designed an experiment in which a small number of acoustically pure sine-waves were combined to produce artificial "replicas" of human speech [22]. Although the recordings contained almost none of the acoustic content associated with natural speech, Remez reported that despite the "unnatural speech quality of the signal...", the "time-varying properties of these... signals are apparently sufficient to support perception of the linguistic message". In other words the experimenters found that modifying the rhythmic properties of these sounds was enough to create a fairly convincing illusion of speech. These findings support Gombrich's suggestion that rhythms produced by even non-vocal sounds may therefore occasionally come to resemble those of speech.

Ernst Gombrich also stated that "Leonardo da Vinci advised young painters to practice their imagination by looking at cracked walls and reading fantastic scenes into strange patches", and even went so far as to assert that "perception is there so that we should know when to *stop* projecting..." (emphasis added) because "...a configuration of sounds evokes some vague association of words and we start projecting them into the medley..." and "then we shall either find that there are other sounds which stand in the way of this projection or we shall be happy until we pass to larger contexts... if then the sense does not fit we must... start introducing some auxiliary hypothesis to save our projection from being confuted by the remaining signposts of sound". The process that Gombrich was describing there will be familiar to mobile phone users as being very similar to that used by technologies which employ predictive texting.

An important lesson of the BBC Monitoring Service experience was that listeners should not be too dogmatic about "saving" a troublesome interpretation. If a monitor sensed victory in finding that he or she seemed to have finally made sense of a particularly incomprehensible utterance, only to be defeated by that apparent meaning being contradicted by sounds that followed, they should not try and force the square peg into a round hole out of sheer frustration. They should instead recognise the long-term value of admitting failure when necessary, and of discarding an incorrect hypothesis, even if much effort had been invested in its formation. They should instead relax, staying true to the axiom that tiny bursts of information are inherently easier to misinterpret than large ones, and trust that their inability to interpret a larger sense indicated that their initial hypothesis had been wrong all along. They should instead formulate a new hypothesis about what these sounds meant, and test the new hypothesis until it too was either discarded or proven. "Rather than pressing the data of sound into our pet projection, we must discard the projection and start again", because "the whole comes before the part".

Medical audiologists refer to the same phenomenon when they advise those who begin to experience partial deafness to (paradoxically) *not* concentrate harder on listening to individual words. On first impressions this advice may seem counterintuitive, but in some cases listeners can benefit from instead relaxing, trying to "go with the flow" and interpret the overall drift rather than the component detail of conversations. Evidently concentrating too hard on minutiæ of unclear sentences can effectively make deafness worse, with the psychological stress produced by hearing problems creating a vicious circle which exacerbates what may originally have only been physical problems. Listeners may in effect worry themselves into focussing on details that, especially in noisy restaurants etc, they might well have missed anyway, without realising that the sentence itself (rather than its individual units) is the richest source of meaningful information. An analogy can be made here with the interpretation of photographs in newspapers. Most people are aware that because newspaper is a poor medium for reproducing subtle shades of grey, photos are broken up into a matrix of tiny black dots (referred to as a "halftone"), whose variations in size collectively simulate the shades of grey present in the original photograph. If one removes a single dot from a halftone composed of hundreds of dots, readers can still interpret the overall image. Similarly if one removes or distorts one syllable in a sentence, readers can still usually interpret that sentence, for instance – "if one removes or distorts one syllable in a sentence, readers can still us*k*ally interpret that sentence".

On a practical note it is worth pointing out however that it is often *normal* to experience hearing difficulties in some social spaces, particularly those bars and clubs etc which look good but sound awful, on account of traditional decor having being replaced with architecturally-chic flat concrete walls, ceilings and floors etc. In many contexts readers can be reassured that hearing problems may be caused by the ignorance some contemporary architects have of building acoustics, and that these problems don't necessarily mean there is anything wrong with your own hearing at all.

All these experiences support the contention of Michael Handel (a historian of military intelligence and deception) that "another piece of advice… based on psychological tests, is not to put too much confidence in conclusions drawn from a very small body of consistent data… because conclusions drawn from very small samples are highly unreliable" [23]. Similarly, to return to our main theme, where the experience of the BBC Monitoring Service was that "six or ten syllables may answer to all sorts of projections, but thirty or forty are less likely to trick you", published EVP recordings often involve no more than three or four syllables.

In an article entitled "Dissecting the Brain with Sound" [24], the *Scientific American* writer Shawn Carlson described an experiment designed by Diana Deutsch, a professor at the University of California, San Diego. Diana Deutsch's experiment demonstrates how acoustic projections can be explored in controlled conditions [25]. Deutsch recorded the sound of a person speaking two neutral words, and created a sequence in which the voice samples are reproduced in alternating stereo channels. Played back over stereo loudspeakers at "dizzying" speeds, fast enough that the sounds remain recognisable as voices while scrambling their semantic content, the sequence produces what Carlson described as "a pattern that sounds like language, but the words are not quite recognisable". Carlson continues "within a few seconds of listening to this strange cacophony, my brain started imposing a shifting order over the chaos as I began hearing distinct words and phrases. First came *blank, blank, blank.*

Then *time, time, time*. Then *no time, long pine* and *any time*. I was then astonished to hear a man's voice spilling out of the right speaker only. In a distinct Australian accent it said *take me, take me, take me*". The ink-blot test invented by Swiss psychiatrist Hermann Rorschach springs to mind, so it is interesting to note that the single Rorschach ink-blot test described in a book by the psychologist Henry Gleitman [26] is described as having evoked not only projections of "a head blowing smoke", but also of a "ghost" and of an "angel" – the last two being themes that strongly resemble the emotional agenda and the imagery that recur throughout EVP research.

One element of the effect produced by Diana Deutsch's recording is described by Jacques Ninio as having been identified by the psychologist Edward Titchener in 1915 [27]. Ninio describes as "verbal satiation" the phenomenon whereby if you rapidly "repeat a word aloud... *house* for example, over and over... soon the sound of the word becomes meaningless... you are puzzled and a little bemused on hearing it". This phenomenon is one that readers can easily test for themselves, and, when listening to Diana Deutsch's recording, it is the *illusion of meaninglessness* produced by such repetitions which the mind attempts to resolve by projecting new meanings onto the apparently abstract voice sounds. In my own experience however, it proved necessary to listen to Diana Deutsch's recording many times before words began to emerge with crystal clarity, but when subjectively 'real' sounding voices did start to form, these illusions were very clear, and the experience was quite unnerving. However, even when concrete and meaningful words have not yet formed, her recording still produces pronounced illusions, since the mind's attempts to impose order on this abstract collage produce a distinct drifting effect in the perceived sound, when the recorded material does in fact not drift, but is instead rigidly unchanging. Diana Deutsch's recording resembles voice manipulation experiments by the sound artist Saul Z'ev, Naeser and Lilly's *Repeating Word Effect* [28], and early experiments by the psychologist BF Skinner [29].

To my amazement it transpired that identical techniques to those employed by Diana Deutsch are also established methods for eliciting EVP, known as "Speech Synthesis" – "a phenomenon which…" according to EVP researcher Raymond Cass "at the present time completely evades physical explanation" [30]. On the strength of demonstrating how acoustic projection effects may explain the mind's ability to misinterpret fragmentary EVP recordings, it can therefore be argued that EVP researchers are in a sense psychologists who have misunderstood their own experiments. However, while it seems likely that many EVP enthusiasts are inadvertently reproducing acoustic projection experiments, it could not conversely be argued that (in emulating the results of Speech Synthesis experiments) Diana Deutsch's recording inadvertently reproduces some kind of supernatural phenomena. This is because the diverse and evolving meanings projected into the unvarying source material of Deutsch's recording by even single listeners demonstrates that the illusions which her experiment generates are endogenous (that they come from inside the listener), and that they are subjective. The pre-emptive narration characteristic of EVP demonstration recordings, which tells listeners in advance what meanings to attach to the sounds that follow, fixes the interpretations that listeners then project, creating an illusion of exogeny (the sense that the meaning comes from outside the listeners) and the illusion that the perceived meaning is shared and therefore objective.

George Miller described an experiment that demonstrates the strength of this prompting effect – the psychologist David Bruce "recorded a set of ordinary sentences and played them in the presence of noise so intense that the voice was just audible but not intelligible". David Bruce then "told his listeners that these were sentences on some general topic – sports, say – and asked them to repeat what they had heard. He then told them that they would hear more sentences on a different topic, which they were also to repeat. This was done several times. Each time the listeners repeated sentences appropriate to the topic announced in advance. When at the end of the experiment Bruce told them that they had heard the same recording every time – all he had changed was the topic they were given – most listeners were unable to believe it" [31][32]. Similarly *Assigned to Listen* argues that "projections have a way of sticking to sound... it isn't easy once you hear your train rattling Carmen to make it change to the Blue Danube". To be fair, the "Speech Synthesis" school of EVP researchers are aware of the phenomenon of acoustic projection [33], and use jumping lock groove vinyl records, magnetic tape and computer sample audio loops, radio static and other sources of repetitive, pseudo random noise as raw material for inducing projections. What seems absent from their understanding of these techniques is however any suggestion that projection effects might be responsible not only for EVP created in these specific ways, but in fact for all interpretations of EVP.

Another auditory projection commonly experienced as a result of listeners being prompted, in this case however by our own memories rather than by any third party, is the illusion, quoted again by Oliver Sacks from a description by neuroscientist and drummer John Iverson – "we tend to hear the sound of a digital clock as *tick tock, tick tock*, even though it is actually *tick, tick, tick, tick*" [34], with, in this case, it being our expectations that cause us to mishear that sound in this specific way, and the same audio illusion was discussed by Ernst Gombrich nearly 50 years earlier [35]. Oliver Sacks goes on to point out that "anyone who has been subjected to the monotonous volleys of noise from the oscillating magnetic fields that bombard one during an MRI has probably had a similar experience..." as "sometimes the deafening ticks of the machine seem to organise themselves into a waltz-like rhythm". Sacks reports similar perceptions to those described by EH Gombrich when he adds that "we tend to add a sort of melody to the sound of a train", and that – in terms of sound art – "there is a wonderful example of this" in the composer Arthur Honegger's masterpiece *Pacific 231*. Sacks also states that we tend to "hear melodies in other mechanical noises" and describes how "one friend of mine feels that the hum of a refrigerator has *Haydn-ish* quality" – such perceptions form the basis of a great deal of contemporary sound art, including my own performance and installation piece *National Grid* [36], although the imagery there has much more to do with acid house than Haydn.

Another illusion which vividly demonstrates the importance of projection in hearing is referred to as the "Picket Fence Effect" by the Canadian psychologist Albert Bregman, and his demonstration of this is more reliable, although arguably less entertaining, than Diana Deutsch's. Albert Bregman recorded spoken sentences "in which half of the sound has been eliminated...", rendered into a kind of staccato effect, "by taking out every other one-sixth (of a) second segment, and replacing it with a silence", before "the same sentence is played with loud noise bursts replacing the silences". In each of these two cases listeners are then asked to "judge the apparent completeness of the sentence" [37]. The fragmented sentences are heard as being virtually incomprehensible; however, when the silent fragments within those recordings have been replaced with white noise, even though it's still hard to fully understand the actual meaning of the sentence, nonetheless the recording is perceived as a smooth stream of unfragmented speech, with the voice appearing to flow continuously underneath and through the bursts of white noise. This flow is completely illusory, produced by the mind projecting familiar and plausible sound-forms onto the white noise, and this illusion can be produced reliably with almost every listener almost every time. Albert Bregman then repeated his experiment with longer silences and longer noise bursts – increasing the duration of each to one-quarter of a second. Because the mind has been supplied within even less information upon which to base any restorative guesswork, a sentence interrupted with longer gaps is therefore less comprehensible, but, amazingly, the same recording interrupted with longer noise bursts is even *easier* to follow.

What Albert Bregman's experiment demonstrates is firstly (and most obviously) again the existence of acoustic projections, but also the fact that although these projections really are illusory, in helping to facilitate the perception of fragmented speech as a continuous flow, under normal circumstances projective illusions actually benefit normal perception, and these illusions help the mind to faithfully represent external reality. Secondly, this experiment shows the importance of contextual information – in this case how the sound of an originally complete and coherent sentence provides, even in badly fragmented form, enough information to enable the mind to interpolate missing fragments, to fill-in the gaps and thereby to perceive more of the perceptual whole. Thirdly and finally, since the white noise used by Albert Bregman to interrupt his sentences is very similar to radio static, his demonstration also shows, again, how adding noise to fragmented voice recordings may paradoxically improve listeners' ability to project meaning onto such recordings.

If however it seems odd that the mind can at least partially interpret streams of sound which have been interrupted by noise better than it can interpret sounds that have been interrupted by silences, in fact there is no paradox, as this makes perfect sense in terms of evolutionary biology. As Bregman puts it "this makes sense ecologically" (the term "ecologically" being used as it's understood in "Gibsonian" psychology as opposed to the more common usage familiar from environmental science) [38]. Bregman states that "silence should not be treated as something that can interrupt a sound", as there is "no physical source in nature that can broadcast silences". In other words, in pre-technological eras it makes sense that we needed to evolve mechanisms to help restore meaningful sound-streams that had been interrupted by for instance an animal cry or the sound of the proverbial twig snapping in a forest etc, and it makes sense that the mind would not have evolved equivalent mechanisms to help restore sound-streams which had been interrupted by silences, because until recently such situations simply did not occur.

In terms of contemporary sound art practice, a related effect is exploited in cinematic sound design. Psychologists RM and RP Warren "asked people to listen to a tape recorded sentence after part of a word had been replaced with the sound of a cough...", and "although part of the word was actually missing, all the participants claimed that they actually heard the entire word and denied that the cough covered part of it". This effect is "more obvious for words in sentences than for words standing alone, is called the phonemic restoration effect" (a phoneme being the smallest segment of speech, for instance syllables like "ba" or "da") [39]. Cinema sound designer David Sonnenschein refers to this effect as resulting from a "law of closure", whereby "the mind will tend to unite two disconnected lines lying along the same trajectory". In practical terms this means that "when a hole or defect occurs in a sound...", for instance when a piece of the magnetic surface flakes-off a recorded tape used in creating the audio track for a film, "a sound editor can hide it by placing another sound over this moment, eg – a car horn". The result is that the movie audience "will perceive that the dialogue continues non-stop", with the mind of the listener "even filling in the actual words that may have been missing from the original track" [40]. Clear analogies exist with this kind of projection and the blind-spot phenomenon (which will be discussed in more detail in a later chapter) and with blinking, as we perceive our visual experiences as more-or-less seamless and continuous through time, and are only occasionally aware of the vast majority of the times that we blink.

Similarly Jacques Ninio quotes from *L'Acoustique*, written by the astronomer and mathematician Rodolphe Radau in 1867, stating that "a very odd phenomenon is the one... referred to by the name of paracousis..." whereby "certain hard of hearing persons who usually do not hear faint sounds, suddenly do hear them when they are accompanied by a loud noise". Radau described the case of "a woman who was always attended by a servant with the job of beating a drum when somebody was talking to her..." who "then heard very clearly", of "another person who heard only when bells were ringing", of "a man who was deaf when one did not beat a nearby bass drum", and of one final individual who "heard best when he was in a carriage that was jolting over the cobblestones". If this reference seems dated, related effects were reported by *The Guardian* in 2002, which described how "noise can improve your hearing" because the "hair cells in the inner ear... are so sensitive they are affected by Brownian motion, the random churning of air molecules". This "stochastic resonance" has an amplifying effect on very faint sounds, and the article went on to say that "computer modelling at the University of Vienna has shown that this constant quiet susurration improves our hearing" to the extent that "we can distinguish sounds about ten times as quiet" as it would be possible for us to hear otherwise [41].

So, referring back to the examples which show how the mind projects meaning into ambiguous, indistinct and incomplete imagery, we need to ask where, in the case of EVP, it is that the raw material of the EVP recordings themselves actually comes from? Signals from across the entire radio spectrum have a tendency to drift away from their original broadcast frequencies, and to spontaneously demodulate onto amplifying circuits, as all audio amplifiers and "gain stages" in radio circuits can function as broadband Very Low Frequency (VLF band) radio receivers. Microphone cables often function as VLF antennas, especially when those cables are unshielded, and when the sound recordings are made out-doors. Taxi transmissions, emergency services, airband, maritime, military, short, medium and long-wave commercial broadcasts, TV voice channels, radio ham experiments,

Rorschach Audio

CB radio, bugging devices, conferencing systems, intercoms, baby alarms and analogue mobile phones all share a tendency to emerge in the same VLF waveband, producing stray signals. These signals are well-known to concert and event PA operators, to technicians who install in-car entertainment systems, and to wildlife recording engineers, who employ an arsenal of electromagnetic shielding devices to eliminate this interference (Faraday cages, electrically conductive tents, paints, coaxial cables, earth lines and grounding etc, and the radio frequency "chokes" or line filters installed in PAs, car stereos and VLF natural phenomena receivers). When stray signals are heard they are often very garbled, and therefore ideal raw material for acoustic projection.

Some EVP researchers say they've attempted to exclude interference from their experimental set-ups, using metal Faraday cages, which surround their equipment, absorbing external radio energy and draining it into the earth. However, another paradox of EVP is that most EVP techniques require not the removal, but the addition of noise to the basic input in order to improve the success of recordings. Radio static, deliberately mistuned voice transmissions (especially in languages not understood by the researchers), audio oscillators, microphone feedback and cassette recordings of foreign language courses and of birdsong, and forms of white noise such as sounds of fountains, hissing taps, rain, surf and wind have all been used. Deliberately adding noise to improve EVP reception may seem counterintuitive, but it makes perfect sense in the light of previous observations. Investigator Raymond

Cass states (among other hypotheses) that EVP voices "may be a mutant development of some remote corner of the subconscious mind, or a transient by product of the electromagnetic pollution which now rings our planet", implying that these explanations are mutually exclusive.

A typical EVP process involves prompting the imagination by asking questions of the deceased entities out loud – in the manner of a Spiritualist séance, recording, and then repeatedly analysing any signals that have emerged, often listening to recorded tapes many times over. EVP researchers allege the presence of polyglot voices, which switch languages from one word to the next, and enthusiasts evidently scour foreign dictionaries for meanings that concur with the rhythms of recorded sequences. EVP researchers maintain that the hypothetical ghosts invent neologisms and take liberties with grammar – in other words we are asked to accept that entities which have the intellect to acquire a grasp of many languages have lost the ability to speak grammatically, and lost the ability to confine themselves to using proper words. These interpretive techniques set the widest possible parameters for the subjective attribution of meaning, thereby accumulating 'data' which would otherwise be disregarded. By asking questions of the spirit world out loud, researchers also tell themselves and other listeners how to interpret sounds before any signals manifest, heavily influencing subsequent interpretations, and encouraging diverse listeners to project shared interpretations in a way that effectively conceals the subjectivity of the interpretive process. Similarly, when compiling EVP demonstration recordings, the convention is to reinforce this process by announcing "meanings" before replaying examples, thereby rendering different listeners' own interpretations useless from the point-of-view of objective analysis. Such prompting features prominently on Raudive's *Breakthrough* recordings, and on the cassettes from which *The Ghost Orchid* CD was compiled, but, even though most of these prompts were edited out at the CD mastering stage, the prompts still survive in the form of printed track titles.

This process of prompting has interesting parallels with the misdirection techniques employed by stage conjurers, card sharps, pickpockets, magicians, ventriloquists and military strategists, many of which involve ingenious uses of sounds (although the most effective misdirection technique employed by conjurors is often the presence of the glamorous assistant). If these forms of prompting are misdirection, important details that EVP researchers also rarely discuss are firstly that "responses" to questions asked in EVP recording sessions are often so quiet as to initially be completely inaudible – only revealing themselves when played back later at very high volume – and secondly that if any "responses" occur at all, they usually emerge only after a very long wait.

The obvious conclusions about the effects of prompting and the role that adding noise seem to play in the perception of EVP are also supported by an experiment designed by psychologists Harald Merckelbach and Vincent van de Ven of Maastricht University [42]. Forty-four undergraduates "were told that the study..." they were about to participate in "was about auditory perception", and "to enhance the credibility of this cover story, they were asked to answer some questions about auditory impairments". They were then "brought into a sound isolated lab room" where "Bing Crosby's *White Christmas* song was playing". "Participants were asked whether they were familiar with the song" and they all "indicated that they were". They were "told that they would hear over headphones a tape with white noise for a three minute period", and that (quote) "the *White Christmas* song that you just heard might be embedded in the white noise below the auditory threshold". The volunteers were asked to press a button if and when they heard the song *clearly*, and "fourteen participants... pressed the button at least once", with this "non-trivial minority" rising from 32% to 35% when the experiment was repeated using a further 108 participants [43], despite the fact that the song "was never presented during the three-minute period". Van de Ven and Merckelbach's experiments show that, in a noisy environment and with the appropriate direction, a significant minority of people can be tricked into hearing specific sounds even when those sounds aren't present and when there is no strong emotional motive, with the implication being that similar effects are likely to be even stronger when, as is the case with EVP, there actually are real sounds and when in some cases there is a very strong emotional motive as well.

Interpreting all this evidence en masse, the implication is that rather than their being anomalous and occasional events, we are unconscious of the extent to which projections take place continuously, as an inherent part of normal perception. For instance it is well-known how difficult it is to spot errors of detail when you're familiar with the overall sense and structure of a written text. Novice readers spell-out individual letters before interpreting each written word, while the eyes of experienced readers glide over text in high-speed "saccadic" jumps. Without analysing and identifying each individual letter, experienced readers sense an overall and generalised structure in the superficial appearance of words, even sentences, sometimes whole paragraphs, and project much of what's seen, as much from memory and from interpolation as from direct sensation. So, the degree of familiarity that comes from having written a text yourself makes it hard for authors to switch off the projecting mechanism and to detect small errors which might lie camouflaged in text that they've written themselves. This explains the necessity, well-known in the publishing industry, for employing professional proof readers (so apologies if this text contains any typographical errors). Similarly with hearing, we actively project sense, interpreting data as conglomerate chunks of meaning, according to pattern recognition techniques which skip from point to point, ignoring some detail in favour of fuzzier, more cost-effective and (most importantly) faster perceptual strategies. The sheer volume of information received by the human senses is so vast that to be overwhelmed by it can not only be confusing, but arguably even medically dangerous, so the mind makes what amounts to intelligent guesses about its environment in order to conserve its two most precious resources – time and effort.

This argument may seem like an exaggeration, because we are only rarely aware of our perceptions being seriously mistaken. However, while I would never suggest that these ideas represent a total theory of all aspects of perception, nonetheless projection represents a metaphorical lift shaft between the unconscious and conscious mind, along which memories of previous experiences are passed, and on top of which important features of consciousness are constructed. Normally projections generate interpretations which agree with an entire spectrum of corroborative inputs from vision, taste, touch, smell, hearing and memory, and therefore we are only aware of the process of projection, and especially its imaginary and subjective aspect, when it occasionally generates images which disagree with the broader context, and it is these errors which we perceive as perceptual illusions.

If the process that produces illusions is the same process that generates perceived reality, it is important to stress firstly that the perceptions generated by projection are for most day-to-day intents and purposes almost entirely accurate representations of the external world, and secondly that the reason they are so accurate is because we invest an immense amount of effort in training our minds to achieve such a high degree of perceptual sophistication. There is an obvious paradox in the fact that experiences we remember are memories of perceptions, and that perceptions themselves are often partially reconstructed memories. This makes the process of providing the mind with the initial training required to acquire the skill of forming accurate projections into an awkward, protracted and complex undertaking, and one which is therefore itself inherently difficult to remember. Although this process does not stop in adult life, much of it can be summarised by the word "play"; and if play is in effect often perceptual training, since much play takes place in early childhood, this may also help explain why so much of early childhood is difficult to remember.

This theory of projective perception traces its origin back to the *Treatise on Physiological Optics* by Hermann Helmholtz, as discussed by the psychologist Richard Gregory [44]. Helmholtz categorised perceptions as unconscious inductive inferences which, despite heavy reliance on memory as well as direct sensation "come about with immutable certainty, lightning speed and without the slightest meditation". Gregory traces the evolution of these ideas to the discovery of the camera obscura, and to the realisation that the images that the brain perceives are not identical to the sensations received by the eyes. The camera obscura and pinhole camera are similar in this respect to the human eye – both being darkened boxes with a hole in one side and a screen on the opposite inside surface. The images received by all these are upside-down. After an image has been sensed by the human retina – upside-down, it is the mind that interprets and in fact completely transforms this image – turning the image back the right way up.

Related phenomena can be explored by experimenting

with coloured glasses – soon after you first wear tinted spectacles, the mind adjusts the appearance of the perceived images to rapidly regain normal colour vision, with the visual perception being modified according to what the mind expects to see. Related phenomena can also be explored using alcohol – since similar processes unify the sensations received by two eyes into a single mental image, but if we are drunk and see double, that is in some respects a more "accurate" picture of what the eyes actually sense, because alcohol can temporarily disrupt the mental process which combines the eyes' two images into a single perception. Helmholtz's research gave rise to the theory of "perceptual hypotheses" – a term which in plain language refers to what amounts to the mind making *intelligent guesses* about the sensations it receives.

In terms of art, the capacity for projection reaches perhaps its ultimate aesthetic realisation in the anamorphoses of Salvador Dalí – his paintings *Paranoiac Visage – the Postcard Transformed*, the *Head of a Woman in the Form of a Battle*, the particularly eerie *Metamorphosis of Hitler's Face into a Moonlit Landscape* and *Portrait of my Dead Brother* [45]. The similarities between these last two paintings and themes in EVP research do not seem accidental, since they all represent personalities that typically haunt the unconscious mind. Jürgenson and Raudive believed they had recorded deceased relatives, and Raudive also thought he had recorded conversations with the ghost of Adolf Hitler, and EVP recordings are littered with alleged contacts with deceased friends, relatives, important historical figures and menacing apparitions of evil personalities whose memories linger in the human imagination. Salvador Dalí was quite rightly kicked out of the Surrealist movement because of his obsession with Adolf Hitler, despite the fact that he was being true to at least one set of Surrealist imperatives – the preoccupation with the dark murmurings of the subconscious mind.

What must be a particularly unnerving aspect of EVP listening is the (apparently common) experience that when first encountered (often accidentally, and as a result of tape recording experiments) stray voices are interpreted as speaking directly to the person who recorded them. The great Surrealist film maker Jean Cocteau exploited this in his deeply mysterious film *Orphée*, suggesting that coded radio messages "inspired by the BBC broadcasts of the occupation" were transmitted from the metaphysical underworld. Orpheus asks Heurtebise "Where could they be coming from? No other station broadcasts them. I feel certain they are addressed to me personally" [46]. It is interesting to note that radio messages sent to French anti-fascists during WW2 used codes which were designed to carry very real and important messages, but to hide those messages within illusions of meaninglessness. Cocteau's "black crepe of little windows is a real sunshine meal", followed by strings of apparently random numerals, seems stylistically faithful. In science, as opposed to art, the hypothesis about Cocteau's imagery is supported by the results of experimentation. Jacques Ninio reports that BF Skinner "prepared recordings of three to five vowels repeated many times" and that "the persons listening to them first thought they heard three to five syllables of an indistinct conversation, then came to believe that they understood what the voice was saying to them..." and that "it concerned their private lives" [47]. Skinner's results also support the findings of David Bruce, in that, as Ninio continues, "the subjects were sure that their descriptions were accurate".

In a survey of the EVP movement written for *Fortean Times* magazine, Jürgen Heinzerling described EVP as "more complex perhaps than even the contradictory abyss that is ufology" [48] and spoke of "field research often hampered by a remarkable lack of critical judgement". Since Jürgen Heinzerling argued, quite rightly, that the scientific community's ignorance of EVP "indirectly supports the spreading of this cult, as potential followers are confronted with convincing demonstrations that are only 'explained' by the quasi-religious musings of the convinced cultists", what I hope to add to this debate is evidence from outside the EVP movement's own findings which places those findings in the context of a viable explanation. While I freely admit that my opinion of EVP is negatively prejudiced, it is not insignificant that while the evidence described here is helpful in understanding EVP, none of it was created in order to criticise EVP, so none of that evidence comes loaded with equivalent preconceptions. My explanatory model posits the evolution of a positive feedback loop in which the emotional appeal of and superstitious predisposition to belief in the afterlife are sufficiently powerful to actively create EVP, and so created, EVP recordings are recycled as evidence of a factual basis on which the belief system then feeds and grows. As a form of psychological test consistent with a concept of *Audio Rorschach*, EVP recordings not only reveal something of the role that emotional factors can play in shaping perceptions, but, as a belief system, EVP also reveals something of the way in which people construct, authenticate and share beliefs, and the way in which social groups gather around ideas.

The advice offered to the BBC Monitoring Service at Evesham, that they should formulate, test, and then either accept, refine or discard projected interpretations, is similar to ideas formulated by the scientific philosopher Karl Popper [49]. Karl Popper propounded the usefulness not of absolute scientific truths (whose fragile, idealised perfections carries with it stylistic echoes of earlier, more primitive beliefs) but of self-refining feedback loops in which "working hypotheses" are progressively formulated, tested, and either discarded or accepted according to rules of experimental evidence. Incidentally Popper's methodology seems to have embodied the same working principles as were embedded in the circuitry of the "Bombes" designed by the mathematician Alan Turing to decipher the Enigma codes of WW2. In a passage that, incidentally, resembles Jean-Paul Sartre's description of how in Jean Genet's poetry "an action passes like an electric current from the subject to the complement" [50], the Alan Turing character depicted in the TV dramatisation of Turing's life spoke of building a "machine which senses contradiction", of how "contradiction implies the solution" and of "electricity…" that "…flows through the hypotheses", in a brief but stunning exposition of this interface between philosophy and electrical engineering. According to Turing's biographer Andrew Hodges [51] the Enigma code-breaking process "depended on the flow of logical implications from a *false* hypothesis" (my emphasis) – a concept which has interesting parallels with recommendations in *Assigned to Listen*.

Since important philosophical ideas are not necessarily either complex or obscure, and since such ideas can (as demonstrated by Turing himself) be embedded in abstract automata as well as in real-world engineering designs, important philosophical ideas can just as easily be embedded in (for instance) sound art. Indeed, the relationship between sound art and philosophy is as ancient as the Pythagorean monochord [52]. As I hope has been demonstrated by this chapter, lessons about scientific methodology can be reverse-engineered by taking a critical interest in styles of pseudo-scientific thought, and, in the case presently under discussion, the entire EVP belief system is a macroscopic false hypothesis (the hypothesis that the dead reveal themselves to us through audio technology), condensed from a larger body of smaller but equally false hypotheses (about the misinterpretation of individual voice recordings). Scientific method itself can be regarded as depending on a flow of logical implications from a whole history of false hypotheses. Indeed understanding perceptual illusions has important ramifications not only for psychology, but also for philosophy of science.

Where Karl Popper's ideas highlight the importance of openly admitting to honest mistakes, this book echoes that point, because some of its content was inspired by a mistake. When compiling the material for the *Ghost Orchid* sleevenotes I attributed advice about psychological projection to authors Olive Renier and Vladimir Rubinstein, who were BBC monitors during WW2. The advice was quoted from a paper entitled *Some Axioms, Musings and Hints on Hearing*, written not by Renier and Rubinstein, but by their Monitoring Supervisor Ernst Gombrich. It was after discovering this mistake that I realised the extent to which investigating the subject of psychological projection could provide tools for analysing sound art as well as for investigating EVP. Indeed, psychological projection is discussed in detail in EH Gombrich's postwar masterpiece *Art and Illusion* [53], and, in this context, it is important to emphasise the influence that Gombrich's wartime intelligence work with *sound* had on a book that is widely regarded as one of the most important works of *visual* art theory ever published.

On a point of historical interest, in practice Ernst Gombrich's role extended beyond interpreting just spoken messages, even in fact to deriving military intelligence from musical broadcasts. According to his obituary writer Charles Hope "it was Gombrich who broke the news to Churchill of the death of Hitler; having recognised the significance of the broadcast of a movement of a symphony of Bruckner written to commemorate the death of Wagner" (in fact this hypothesis was one of several proposed by Gombrich to Churchill as potential explanations for the Bruckner broadcast) [54]. On another point of historical interest, as described earlier, the BBC Monitoring Service employed poets, linguists and refugees from Hitler and Franco, including Spanish Republican Arturo Barea and (his wife) the Austrian journalist Ilse Kulcsar [55], who wrote and translated the book *La Llama*, whose English edition has a name that'll be familiar to music fans – The Clash [56] ("The hillsides ring with "*Free the People*", or can I hear the echo from the days of '39?... Spanish bombs on the Costa Brava, I'm flying in on a DC10 tonight").

In *Art and Illusion* EH Gombrich cites Leonardo da Vinci's famous advice to novice painters, which is particularly interesting because of its final sentence. "You should look at certain walls stained with damp, or at stones of uneven colour. If you have to invent some backgrounds you will be able to see in these the likeness of divine landscapes, adorned with mountains, ruins, rocks, woods, plains, hills and valleys in great variety: and then again you will see there battles and strange figures in violent action, expressions of faces and clothes and an infinity of things which you will be able to reduce to their complete and proper forms. In such walls the same thing happens as in the sound of bells, in whose stroke you may find every named word you can imagine". The phenomena Leonardo describes are acoustic projections closely related to the experiments cited and to EVP. What is most surprising is that while the historic influence of Leonardo's advice with respect to figurative and abstract painting is probably inestimable, from the point of view of fine art practice, his final sentence seems to have been almost totally ignored.

Diana Deutsch's contention that "Leonardo may have

been particularly susceptible to such transformations…" because "perhaps this facility is associated with extreme creativity" [57] needs to be balanced with the understanding that the processes which create such mishearings are, although certainly creative, not unusual. These faculties are instead aspects of normal perception that are not confined to individuals like Leonardo. As the quotation from "London Bells" reproduced at the beginning of this chapter clearly shows [58], they're common enough to have been immortalised in vernacular folklore. Indeed, according to popular legend, four times Lord Mayor Dick Whittington was called back to London by a message he believed he'd heard in the sound of church bells.

With regard to Gombrich's *Art and Illusion* focussing its discourse primarily on forms of visual art such as painting, drawing and sculpture, acknowledging the role that psychological projection plays in the appreciation of such art-forms explains at least two common responses to experiencing artworks. The first is the much parodied tendency, often annoying to members of the public, for chin-stroking critics to gaze fixedly at a work of pretentious contemporary art and ask "yes, but what does this mean?" While the process of reading meanings into "difficult" art may sometimes be taken to ridiculous extremes, the present discourse suggests that original art provokes its audience into consciously articulating questions which the mind continually asks of its environment anyway. The mind effectively asks "what does this mean?" every time it encounters and identifies any visual, auditory or even tactile sense-object. So, in that sense, the tendency to search for meanings in art is as natural as it is unavoidable and in fact also necessary, and the skill of contemporary artists is in bringing that response to the surface, and in subjecting aspects of the underlying process to conscious examination. The second response (which tends to rile artists rather than members of the public) is the tendency for critics to flatter themselves that work which an artist considers original "reminds them of…" such-and-such, that the critic saw or heard somewhere else before. Again, this is a normally unconscious reflex whose conscious articulation has been provoked by the artwork, and artists can rest assured that the statements it produces are usually at least trite if not necessarily meaningless, because every perception that adults are able to make sense of, by virtue of having been made sense of, necessarily reminds them of *something*. As the saying goes – "everyone's a critic", and apparently Goethe believed that true poetry lies not in the provision of authentically new experiences, but in stimulating the recollection of memories, which in this case, left to their own devices the would-be critics would have happily forgotten.

In *Art and Illusion* EH Gombrich also mentions his personal friendship with Karl Popper, and if the influence that the ideas of Popper and of the mathematician and information theorist Claude Shannon had on *Art and Illusion* lends credence to fashionable rhetoric about relationships between science and art, then Popper's preoccupation with methodology highlights significant shortcomings in some areas of fine arts practice. If it can be argued that EVP researchers assume their experiments are scientific, primarily because the machines used in their laboratories visually resemble scientific apparatus (while their working methods often render their results scientifically meaningless), then this highlights the importance of understanding the differences between science and technology, and those between scientists and inventors. Technology and science are not synonymous. Technology is usually the product of science, but sometimes it is not. Similarly inventors are not always scientists. Technology can be invented by individuals who do not make use of scientific methodology, and who are therefore not strictly speaking scientists. It is true that many scientists have developed hypotheses after experiencing dramatic flashes of "irrational", unsystematic, intuitive, creative (and therefore by implication "artistic") insight, but what makes them scientists is the time, effort and expertise that they invested in proving that their hypotheses were justified.

In previous publications I have argued that while art is not necessarily science, science is always art [59], but many of the artists involved in projects intended to promote public understanding of links between art and science seem instead to have been concerned with what it would be more accurate to describe as links between art and technology. The danger of this over-emphasis on technology is that it may produce art which, like EVP experiments, superficially resembles scientific experiments, but which is in some respects little more than scientifically meaningless (and which in some cases even promotes the public misunderstanding of science).

It is critical for genuinely scientific researchers to for instance reference the sources from which the ideas and information they use have been drawn, and this criterion alone represents a measure by which it is possible to see that some of those who talk about art and science have learned very little from their exposure to scientific thought (and this is especially pertinent when it comes to those artists and researchers who have used, and will no doubt continue to use, the *Rorschach Audio* project itself as the unacknowledged blueprint for their own artworks and fundraising initiatives).

From their perspectives in art and science Karl Popper and EH Gombrich both stressed the importance of not developing a strong attachment to a hypothesis after it has proven to be false. Both emphasised the value of admitting to mistakes and of moving on to revised or new hypotheses when necessary. Without getting drawn into too much discussion of this fascinating person, the philosopher Freddie Ayer argued that while metaphysical statements may well have "meaning" (and I should add, sometimes great beauty) in the sense that they have emotional appeal, nonetheless all metaphysical statements are inherently and literally meaningless, because they are statements that can be proven neither true nor false [60]. This author's interest in auditory and visual illusions is reflected in Ayer's interest in what amount to linguistic illusions. Incidentally, Ayer was also a military intelligence officer liaising with French resistance fighters during WW2, and was involved with just the kind of radio traffic that the imagery in *Orphée* drew upon [61].

Such thinking about scientific method is echoed in the writings of the Cambridge pathologist Ian Beveridge, who discussed those who "question everything they are told and (who) frequently rebel against the conventional" [62], by which he meant scientists, who stated that a "hypothesis is sometimes very fruitful without being correct" [63], but who warned against developing "parental affection" for such false hypotheses [64]. Such "parental affection" is for artists and scientists the equivalent of the emotional appeal that Freddie Ayer implied draws people to believe in metaphysical statements. It is the need to come up with new ideas, even if those ideas are patently false, this affection, and the emotional appeal of EVP which still seduce some artists into literally believing EVP. The Swedish sound-artist Carl Michael von Hausswolff for instance has undertaken the archiving and exhibiting of EVP researcher Friedrich Jürgenson's work; and, while there are many reasons why someone might wish to do that, when asked "do you believe in the phenomena of EVPs... do ghosts exist?" Hausswolff replied "I don't think it's of any interest if I believe in these things or not, what I find interesting is the fact that more and more people, these days seem to say No to a lot of things", and stated that "they don't believe in UFOs, they don't believe in things that they cannot touch, they don't believe in life after death, etc, if we were complaining about the materialistic society in the 70s – look at this place now, it's a disaster", before flatly contradicting his earlier statement by concluding that "of course I believe in EVP, it's fantastic!" [65].

During a lecture at The Royal Institution [66] the chemist Carl Djerassi expressed a wish to puncture the assumption, apparently made by a former winner of the art world's flagship award the Turner Prize, that arts-science interactions are in any way enriched by the stimulus of mutual misunderstanding between these fields. Djerassi's statement should be a timely reminder of the level of integrity that history (if not expediency) demands. Unless artists are willing to learn from their mistakes, the only cause such misunderstandings serve is the cause of ignorance. My ultimate (and admittedly idealistic) hope is that the situation may arise where artists not only learn from interactions with scientific ideas, but where they begin to reciprocate by making practical, direct contributions to science. While this objective may not have been achieved by this project as such, what I am prepared to argue is that *Rorschach Audio* has at least contributed to actively promoting the public understanding of science.

Karl Popper stated that "there are no uninterpreted sense data" [67], while EH Gombrich asserted that "there is no reality without interpretation", and that "just as there is no innocent eye, there is no innocent ear" [68], so I draw this chapter towards a conclusion by agreeing with what I believe is an idea developed and shared by Helmholtz, Gombrich, Gregory and others, that at a fundamental neurological level many of the faculties exercised in basic forms of perception, in the formulation of scientific hypotheses, and in the appreciation of art have a great deal in common.

Speaking as someone who has recently experienced

this, I also agree with Richard Gregory's observation that during bereavement "sights and sounds are commonly misperceived as evidence of... (the) return" of the deceased [69], and I am certain many readers will confirm, with a nod to Goethe, that such perceptions can be profoundly moving and beautiful. Gregory's observation can be offered as a global explanation for EVP – phenomena which are, in my opinion and to paraphrase Freddie Ayer, emotionally significant, but, in the strictest factual sense, virtually meaningless. So, finally, if the style and content of this chapter seem a harsh appraisal of phenomena whose creative impetus we know stems from an instinct that we all share – namely the desire to triumph over the tragedy of human mortality and to retain contact with lost friends – then I would like to suggest that the fundamental message of any statement which undermines faith in the afterlife remains, as always, the same. That message is the most romantic notion that humans ever conceived, and is advice that remains profound no matter how clichéd it becomes – seize the day.

[1] Justin Chatburn & Mike Harding (editors) *The Ghost Orchid – An Introduction to EVP* Ash International PARC CD1, 1999 – *The Ghost Orchid* has been reprinted three times since first publication, and contains Konstantin Raudive's original *Breakthrough* recordings alongside material recorded by EVP researcher Raymond Cass, as well as the CD sleevenotes containing the first *Rorschach Audio* text

[2] Friedrich Jürgenson *Rösterna Från Rymden* Saxon & Lindström, Stockholm, 1964

[3] Friedrich Jürgenson *Sprechfunk Mit Verstorbenen* Hermann Bauer KG, Freiburg, 1967

[4] Friedrich Jürgenson *Radio och Mikrofonkontakt med de Döda* Nybloms, Uppsala, 1968

[5] Mike Harding & CM von Hausswolff "1485.0 kHz" *Cabinet Magazine*, New York, Winter 2000, pp.56-61

[6] Konstantin Raudive *Breakthrough* Colin Smythe, Gerrards Cross, 1971 (also Taplinger, New York 1971)

[7] *The Unexplained: Mysteries of Mind, Space & Time* (French edition *L'Inixpliqué*) was a partwork magazine created by Orbis publishing in the 1980s, which investigated mysteries such as the Bermuda Triangle, UFOs, Bigfoot, ESP etc; details are uncertain at the time of writing, but the *Breakthrough* flexidisc may have been published to accompany an article called "Whispers of Immortality" by Frank Smyth, which the *Fortean Times* website states was published in *The Unexplained* vol.2, p.418 "c.1980" – my recollection is that this flexidisc was published in 1982, either way however these recordings are reproduced in full on *The Ghost Orchid*

[8] Oliver Sacks *Seeing Voices* Picador, London, 1991, pp.5-6
[9] David Wright *Deafness – A Personal Account* Stein and Day, New York, 1969, quoted in Sacks, op.cit.
[10] Helen Phillips "They Do It With Mirrors" *New Scientist*, 17 June 2000
[11] H McGurk & J MacDonald "Hearing Lips and Seeing Voices" *Nature* 264, 1997, pp.746-748
[12] Jens Bernsen *Lydd i Design* Delta Akustik & Vibration / Dansk Design Centre, Copenhagen, 1999, p.93, and personal experience
[13] Colin Cherry "Some Experiments on the Recognition of Speech" *Journal of Acoustical Society of America* 25, vol.5, 1953, pp.975-979
[14] Barry Arons "A Review of the Cocktail Party Effect" MIT Media Lab PDF, 1992
[15] Primo Levi *The Periodic Table* Abacus, London, 1986, p.55
[16] Olive Renier & Vladimir Rubinstein *Assigned to Listen* BBC, 1986, pp.75-79
[17] Simon Calder "The Odd Weekend with Auntie" *The Independent* (Long Weekend Supplement) 3 May 1997, p.16 – "Auntie" is an anachronistic British nick-name for the BBC
[18] Maggie Brown "Watch on the World" *The Guardian*, Media Supplement, 1 October 2001, pp.6-7
[19] http://www.subbrit.org.uk/rsg/sites/w/woodnorton/ – retrieved 1 Sept 2008
[20] Olive Renier & Vladimir Rubinstein, op.cit., p.13
[21] Leonard Miall "Oliver Whitley" obituary,

The Independent, 24 March 2005

[22] RE Remez, PE Rubin, DB Pisoni & TD Carrell "Speech Perception Without Traditional Speech Cues" *Science* 212, 1981, pp.947-949

[23] Michael Handel "Intelligence and Deception" in John Gooch & Amos Perlmutter (editors) *Military Deception and Strategic Surprise* Frank Cass, London, 1982, p.138

[24] Shawn Carlson "Dissecting the Brain with Sound" *Scientific American*, December 1996, pp.80-83

[25] Diana Deutsch *Musical Illusions and Paradoxes* Philomel Records CD 001, La Jolla 1995, tracks 5 & 6

[26] Henry Gleitman "Perceptual Hypotheses" in *Psychology* Norton, London 1986, pp.203-204

[27] Jacques Ninio *The Science of Illusions* Cornell University Press, 2001, p.32 (originally *La Science des Illusions* Editions Odile Jacob, Paris, 1998)

[28] MA Naeser & JC Lilly "Repeating Word Effect" *Journal of Speech & Hearing Research*, 1971

[29] Jacques Ninio, op.cit., p.33

[30] Raymond Cass, narration transcribed from original cassettes used for compiling *The Ghost Orchid* CD

[31] George Miller *The Psychology of Communication* Penguin, London, 1967, pp.79-80

[32] David Bruce "Effects of Context on the Intelligibility of Heard Speech" quoted in Colin Cherry (editor) *Information Theory* Butterworths, London, 1956, pp.245-252

[33] Leonard Lander "Audiomancy" in *Beyond The Dial* Trapezohedron Press, Wasa, 2000

[34] Oliver Sacks *Musicophilia* Picador, London, 2007, p.243
[35] EH Gombrich *Art and Illusion* Phaidon, London, 1960, p.307
[36] Disinformation *Stargate / National Grid / Theophany* Ash International Ash 3.2 LP, 1996, plus *National Grid* sound installations at The Museum of Installation, 1997, Kettle's Yard, 2000, Fabrica Gallery, 2001 etc
[37] Albert Bregman & Pierre Ahad *Demonstrations of Auditory Scene Analysis* CD, The MIT Press, 1990, track 31
[38] Albert Bregman *Auditory Scene Analysis* The MIT Press, 1990, pp.373-378 – the effect in question is based on a phenomenon independently discovered by Miller & Lidlicker in 1950 (Bregman p.752) and by Giovanni Vicario in 1960 (Bregman p.759)
[39] RM Warren & RP Warren "Auditory Illusions and Confusions" *Scientific American* 223, 1970, pp.30-36 – quoted in Stephen Kosslyn & Robin Rosenberg *Psychology* Pearson, 2004, p.157
[40] David Sonnenschein *Sound Design* Michael Wiese Productions, Los Angeles, 2001, p.81
[41] David Hambling "Sound Effects – Noise Can Improve Your Hearing" *The Guardian*, 28 March 2002
[42] Harald Merckelbach & Vincent van de Ven "Another White Christmas" *Journal of Behavior Therapy & Experimental Psychiatry*, 32, 2001, pp.137-144
[43] Vincent van de Ven & Harald Merckelbach "The Role of Schizotypy, Mental Imagery and Fantasy Proneness in Hallucinatory Reports of Undergraduate Students" *Personality & Individual Differences* 35, 2003, pp.889-896

[44] RL Gregory "Perception as Hypotheses" in *The Oxford Companion to the Mind* Oxford University Press, 1987, pp.608-611, see also the entry on Hermann Helmholtz, pp.308-310

[45] Robert Descharnes & Gilles Néret *Dalí* Taschen, Cologne, 1997

[46] Carol Martin-Sperry (translator) *Cocteau* Viking, New York, 1972, pp.101-191

[47] Jacques Ninio, op.cit., p.33

[48] Jürgen Heinzerling "All about EVP" *Fortean Times* 104, London, November 1997, pp.26-30

[49] EH Gombrich, op.cit., pp.271-272

[50] Jean-Paul Sartre *Saint Genet – Actor and Martyr* translated by Bernard Frechtman, WH Allen, London, 1964, p.436

[51] Andrew Hodges *Turing* Phoenix, London, 1997, p.26, for a more detailed explanation of this idea see Andrew Hodges *Alan Turing – The Enigma* Vintage, London, 1992, pp.179-183

[52] Joe Banks *The Rumble* exhibition catalogue, The Royal Society of British Sculptors (since re-named The Royal British Society of Sculptors) London, 2001, p.2

[53] EH Gombrich, op.cit.

[54] Charles Hope "Sir Ernst Gombrich" (obituary) *The Independent*, 6 Nov 2001

[55] Arturo Barea (author) & Ilsa Barea (translator) *The Forging of a Rebel* Walker, New York, 2001 (reprinting Arturo Barea *The Clash* Faber & Faber, 1946)

[56] Olive Renier *Before the Bonfire* Drinkwater, 1984, p.100

[57] Diana Deutsch, correspondence of 17 August 2000

[58] Geoffrey Grigson (editor) *The Cherry Orchard* Phoenix House, London, 1959, p.296

[59] Joe Banks, op.cit.

[60] AJ Ayer *Language, Truth and Logic* Victor Gollancz, London, 1936

[61] Ben Rogers *AJ Ayer – A Life* Vintage, London, 2000, pp.182-183

[62] WIB Beveridge *The Art of Scientific Investigation*, Heinemann, London, 1950, p.46

[63] WIB Beveridge, op.cit., pp.48-49

[64] WIB Beveridge, op.cit., p.140

[65] CM von Hausswolff (interview) *Sound Projector* 10, London, 2002

[66] Carl Djerassi, Dennis Rosen Memorial Lecture, The Royal Institution, 30 June 2000

[67] Karl Popper *Unended Quest* Routledge, London, 1994, p.161

[68] EH Gombrich, op.cit., p.307

[69] RL Gregory *The Oxford Companion to the Mind* op.cit., pp.79-80

Acknowledgments

Personal thanks to Song-Ming Ang, Knut Aufermann, Colette Bailey, Alex Barrett, Tim Blackwell, Caroline Banks, Colin Banks, Steve Barfield, Angus Carlyle, Kim Cascone, Justin Chatburn, Louise Clements, Andrew Clifford, Nic Collins, David Cunningham, Peter Cusack, Chris Daley, Ross Dalziel, Poulomi Desai, Diana Deutsch, Gareth Farry, Bronac Ferran, Gregg Fisher, Rob Flint, Lynne Freeman, Michaela Freeman, Chris French, Graham Frost, Charlie Gere, Ernst Gombrich, Olga Goriunova, Geoffrey Grigson, Sophie Grigson, Christopher Grinbergs, Saner Gursel, Barry Hale, Dianne Harris, Graham Harwood, Janis Jeffries, Ryan Jordan, Rahma Khazam, Magz Hall, Phil Hallett, Mike Harding, Paul Lansdowne, Cathy Lane, Ingrid Leary, Rita Leppiniemi, Peter Lewis, Alex McLean, Adam Lowe, Matthew Miller, Marianne Mulvey, Makiko Nagaya, Jane Parsons, Chris Patten, Tatiana Patten, Mark Pilkington, Ed Pinsent, Paul Purgas, Gavin Ramsey, James Register, Peter Ride, Simon Schaffer, Sharon Sinclair, Claire Staunton, Jonathan Swain, Claire Szulc, Tony White, Liz Whitehead, Julie Warrington, Alex Warwick, Celia Woolf, Maria X and to all at the AHRC, for providing information, advice, or help with organising *Rorschach Audio* exhibits, fundraising, lectures and publications etc.

Thanks to The Anomalistic Psychology Research Unit (London), The Arts & Humanities Research Council, Ash International, The Barbican Centre (London), The British Council, The Broadway Cinema (Nottingham),

The Central School of Speech and Drama (London), Brighton Cinematheque, Dorkbot (London chapter), Fabrica (Brighton), FACT (Liverpool), Hull School of Art and Design, Hull Time Based Arts, Inheritance Projects (London), The Institute for Modern and Contemporary Culture, Kinetica Museum (London), Leonardo Music Journal, London College of Communication, MUU (Helsinki), Nottingham Trent University Fine Art Department, Palais de Tokyo (Paris), Quad (Derby), Radio New Zealand, The Royal British Society of Sculptors (London), The School of The Art Institute of Chicago, Slash Seconds, The Sonic Arts Network, Space Studios (London), Usurp Art Gallery (London), T1&2 Gallery (London) and Vitamin S (Auckland).

PROJECT HISTORY

Rorschach Audio publications include *The Ghost Orchid* CD sleevenotes, PARC / Ash International, 1999, pp.16-20; "Rorschach Audio – A Lecture by Joe Banks at The Royal Society of British Sculptors" *Diffusion* 8, Sonic Arts Network, August 2000, pp.2-6; "Rorschach Audio – Ghost Voices and Perceptual Creativity" *Leonardo Music Journal*, vol.11, The MIT Press, 2001, pp.77-83; "Rorschach Audio – Art and Illusion for Sound" *Strange Attractor Journal*, vol.1, 2004, pp.124-159; "Audio Rorschach" Earshot, UKISC, August 2007, pp.26-33; "Rorschach Audio & the Cemetery of Sound – Electronic Voice Phenomena & Sonic Archives" *Slash Seconds* 8, Leeds Metropolitan University, April 2008 (online journal); "Rorschach Audio

– All Aboard!" in Song-Ming Ang & Kim Cascone (editors) *The Book of Guilty Pleasures* Circadian Songs, 2011, pp.12-13; and an untitled article about visual illusions in *The Starry Rubric Set* publication, Wysing Arts Centre / An Endless Supply, Cambridge, 2011.

Artworks produced in context of this research project include two *Rorschach Audio* sound works exhibited in the "Moths to / from a Flame" exhibition by Makiko Nagaya, James Early and Johnny Vivash, at T1&2 Gallery, London, September 2008; the soundtrack (prepared in collaboration with Mark Pilkington) for the *Rorschach Audio* exhibition at Goldsmiths College, London, December 2008; the *Rorschach Audio – Orpheus Mix* commissioned by Palais de Tokyo, Paris, July 2009; the *Rorschach Audio – Projective Apperception Test* commissioned by MUU Helsinki and published on the *MUU For Ears* CD, vol.3, 2010; the *Rorschach Audio* soundtrack exhibited alongside *The Origin of Painting* sound and light installation at Usurp Gallery, London, January to March 2008; and the *Sound Portrait of Jean Genet* and *Let Him Have It Chris!* artworks, first published on Flickr, 14 September 2011 (all these artworks are attributed to Disinformation, the Goldsmiths and Usurp shows were Disinformation solo exhibitions).

Popular Wireless Weekly, August 26th, 1922.

PSYCHIC PHENOMENA AND WIRELESS.

*Note: Mr. Risdon has written an impartial review of the theory that wireless may possibly assist in effecting communication with the spirit world, believed to exist by psychic investigators. This article must be regarded purely from a scientific standpoint. The theory is an interesting one, and no such has been discussed considerably both in this country and in America. POPULAR WIRELESS expresses no opinion on the subject, and Mr. Risdon's article is in the nature of a statement setting forth the scientific aspect of a theory lately propounded by Sir Arthur Conan Doyle and others.—*EDITOR.

By P. J. RISDON, F.R.S.A.

IT is not unnatural that the now universal interest in wireless should lead to the question, "Will wireless constitute a means of communication with the departed?"

A well-known spiritualist has expressed the view that wireless is going to be of assistance in this respect, and bases his opinion on a theory that spirits are vibrations of the ether. If they are, there appears to be no reason why their images should not be recorded on photographic plates—that is one of the successes claimed by him—and if their images can be thus received, communication by means of other ether vibrations—namely, wireless—does not at first sight seem beyond the bounds of possibility, always supposing that spirits are familiar with and susceptible to such vibrations.

There is no proven means of judging as to whether electro-magnetic waves would constitute the means of such communications, or whether some other form of wireless apparatus, capable of transmitting and receiving other vibrations, such as those of telepathy, would need to be evolved.

Moreover, since the existence of the ether itself is, though largely accepted for the purpose of certain scientific conclusions, not actually proven, it is impossible to discuss these difficulties conclusively until these difficulties have been considered and resolved.

It will probably be better, however, to discuss them impartially and from different points of view.

Innate in every human being is a constraint to recognise a Supreme Power responsible for the natural order of things—for every event in the universe. It matters not whether it be a case of religious upbringing or that of a poor savage "whose untutored mind sees God in clouds or hears Him in the winds." An equally spontaneous and universal belief is that the body is but a temporary abode of a soul that cannot die, even although it must suffer eclipse in a worldly sense.

It may be argued that these two beliefs prove nothing, and that they are due to "the wish being father to the thought."

The only reply to such a contention is that they are universal, and independent of any religious doctrine or belief, and of education and will-power; that they constitute, directly or indirectly, the mightiest force in human affairs, and, moreover, that the second, if not the first, is sine qua non in respect of the subject under consideration.

Although, on the one hand, we find certain religious faiths nominally opposed to psychic research—i.e., the investigation of phenomena, real or apparent, that do not fall under any of the other recognised sciences—on the other hand, many extremely religious persons, who are not spiritualists, are firm believers in manifestations, such as visitations from relatives with whom they have communion, and the Bible itself is rich in support of such experiences, whence it is difficult to see why honest

research and investigation should be condemned as contrary to the precepts of true religion. The more deeply one explores the realms of science, the more one is impressed and sobered by the wonders revealed.

There appears to be nothing inherently impossible in the conception of a spirit world, or in that of departed spirits communicating with the living. And if from the army of "spiritualists" we weed out the impostors, we still have left a few who are generally regarded as sane men of unimpeachable integrity, and whose testimony leaves us little choice but to believe that strange manifestations take place for which no conclusive scientific explanation is as yet forthcoming.

Normal and Abnormal.

Briefly, the creed of "Spiritualism" is that death merely opens the portal to another stage of existence in a sphere of which that portion nearest the world is denoted as the "Astral Plane," whence departed spirits can communicate with those left behind. It is a very ancient creed, probably as old as any religion.

Included in the alleged experiences of spiritualists are [obscured by watermark] of coloured emanations from a human being, the [obscured] being supposed to [obscured] [obscured] a person is supposed to leave the body and become visible beside it, returning to it when the spell is broken.

The theory of Transmigration of Souls is that after death the spirit assumes another bodily form according to its deserts. Thus, a person of certain evil habits may take the form of a worm or of some other lowly creature, and undergo another course of evolution before he gets his chance again. It is claimed that this occurrence is part retribution for wrong-doing, and the belief in reincarnation is largely held in India and the East.

It is quite possible for a person, other than a certified lunatic, either to dream or to imagine the occurrence of events that do not actually take place. And it must be remembered that the normal shades imperceptibly into the abnormal.

Possible Use of Valves.

Whatever the source and means of propagation may be, hypnotism is a power which certain persons are unquestionably capable of exercising over others to such an extent that the subject loses his mental identity, and the merest suggestion ensures immediate and entire obedience. That this power has been grossly abused is common knowledge.

By telepathy is meant the transmission of thought images, or sensations from one mind to another, independently of conscious voice or will-power, and irrespective of distance. Such experiences are so common that it is unnecessary to give instances. Premonition of an impending event may possibly be due to telepathy, although some prefer to class it as a communication from a spirit world. We

shall presently have more to say about telepathy.

It is stated that Dr. Baraduc has already satisfied himself, as the result of experiments, that thought waves are projected by human beings, and, if this be true, there is nothing impossible in the suggestion that instruments, corresponding in their function to that of the thermionic valve, may be invented for magnifying such thought waves, either for transmission or reception or for both.

In this connection may be mentioned an invention of the late Dr. Waller, which has an important bearing upon the subject. The writer spent many hours with the doctor in his laboratory investigating and testing the apparatus which faithfully records, by rapid changes in the electrical resistance of the human body, the effects of thought and sensation.

The Sub-conscious Mind.

If we are to believe the evidence of our senses, we are forced to the conclusion that every normal person possesses a dual mind; the conscious and sub-conscious.

The conscious mind is that which regulates and governs [obscured by watermark] the sub-conscious [obscured] [obscured by watermark] [obscured] conscious and occasionally, but not always, the conscious is apparently capable of [obscured]

[obscured] asked [obscured] [obscured] many [obscured] [obscured] imparts that is it not imperceptible, although we know it is there; then we may we cannot remember. The next day—or it may be a long time afterwards, when the incident is forgotten—the sub-conscious mind suddenly and unexpectedly imparts the desired information.

If we may so express it, the sub-conscious mind lies quiescent but ever on the watch, as, when the conscious mind becomes vacant, takes possession. I leave home daily, enter a train and go to my office; but my active mind is in the ascendant. I do not consciously think of the office, but my sub-conscious mind directs my footsteps there.

Not Proven.

Walking in one's sleep may be another instance of the exercise of the sub-conscious mind, unless it be attributable to purely galvanic action. The sub-conscious mind receives and stores impressions, and it is probably the transmitting and receiving station for telepathic phenomena.

Quite distinct from the dual mind is multiple personality—the existence in the same body of two entirely different identities or personalities. It is stated that there is medical evidence of cases where there has been a prolonged struggle between two such identities for possession, resulting in one ousting the other. This may or may not be true; if it be true, it has an important bearing on the subject generally. It must not be confused with ordinary conflicting emotions that everyone (unless devoid of conscience) experiences when about to take some step that his better nature proclaims as unworthy.

Chapter 2
Burning an Illusion

"When the mist's a rising
And the rain is falling
And the wind is blowing cold across the moor
I hear the voice of my darling
The girl I loved and lost a year ago
Johnny remember me
Well it's hard to believe I know
But I hear her singing in the sighing of the wind
Blowin' in the tree tops way above me"
– John Leyton & The Outlaws *Johnny Remember Me* 1961

"Burnin' all illusion tonight" – Bob Marley

The relationship between sound and allegedly supernatural phenomena is almost certainly as old as superstition itself. Indeed, probably the most culturally pervasive, strongly mimetic and instantly recognisable representation of the ghostly form depicts the disembodied human soul as a nebulous and indistinct translucent white shape, which drifts around a room, accompanied by the sound of wailing. Certainly this image has been influenced by the idea of people playing at being ghosts, by, typically, cutting two large eye-holes in a white bed sheet and running round at night, making ghostly sounds for fun, but that image itself seems to be based on earlier precedents. *The Oxford*

Companion to the Mind, edited by the great experimental psychologist Richard Gregory, offered the hypothesis that the reason conventional representations of ghosts have this characteristic form is because that form derives from the anthropomorphisation of after-images produced on the retina by candle flames and by light seen entering dark bedrooms through key-holes at night. These after-images "appear very much larger when the gaze is transferred onto a distant wall", and there is a strong tendency for the mind to "see" human forms "in even quite random shapes" [1]. What Gregory did not mention however, was that the visual image typically associated with ghosts is critically animated not only by the beliefs and superstitions of the people perceiving it, but also by sound – specifically by the sound of wailing wind, which is, by an equivalent process, anthropomorphised and mis-perceived as though it was the ghost's actual voice (and I know from childhood experience that the sound of wind whistling across the top of a chimney in an old dark house can be scary enough, even without attendant visual imagery and without "believing" in ghosts).

So, in that context, it is perhaps not surprising that equivalent illusions and misperceptions of sound continue to follow, to (so-to-speak) "track", and to adapt to changes in their cultural environment, and that in doing so these mishearings acquire their own cultural history. While there have been many other, more ad-hoc precedents and similar beliefs, the idea that perceptions of ghostly activity might be systematically interpreted as factual evidence supporting an actual belief system, was most effectively formalised in 1848, with the birth of the Spiritualist movement. Sisters Kate, Margaret and their older sister (and subsequent business manager) Leah Fox, announced their alleged contact with the ghost of a murdered tradesman in Hydesville, New York, who they claimed communicated with the younger sisters by making rapping sounds on the underside of a table [2]. The Fox sisters became a media sensation, with the publicity they attracted giving rise to organised Spiritualism. Indeed, the appeal of the Spiritualist movement proved so enduring that when, 40 years later, they admitted their supernatural communications had been a hoax, Spiritualism "continued as if the confessions of the Fox sisters had never happened" [3].

It seems obvious that the reason original Spiritualism survived the self-debunking of its own evidential basis was because of the sheer strength of the emotional appeal of the underlying beliefs. Death, if not actual ghosts, haunts us all, so beliefs that offer any possibility that death might be any kind of illusion command an appeal so magnetic as to account for little short of virtually the entire history of (organised and disorganised) religion. So, just as religion itself continues to constitute a potent force throughout society, despite the influence of science on contemporary modes of thought, it is no less surprising that (memetically speaking) Spiritualist beliefs also try to keep pace with cultural changes, and try to integrate themselves into society's evolving belief systems as well. Today the primary manifestation of that tendency is the so-called Electronic Voice Phenomena movement, founded around 1960. The EVP movement's followers make use of radio, microphone and tape recording technology etc, to record sounds which EVP enthusiasts believe are literally the voices of phantoms, spirits, poltergeists, dead people – of real ghosts.

Implausible as this might sound, one of the reasons that the EVP movement commands a consistent level of public interest, is because EVP researchers find themselves in surprisingly respectable company, not least that of Thomas Alva Edison (1847-1931), the former telegraph operator who went on (among many achievements) to improve (rather than to invent) the incandescent light-bulb and to invent the phonograph. *Scientific American* correspondent Martin Gardner maintains that "in his youth Edison was an outspoken freethinker", and quotes a *New York Times* interview of 2 October 1910 in which, to a storm of opposition from religious commentators, Thomas Edison stated that "there is no more reason to believe that any human brain will be immortal, than there is to think that one of my phonograph cylinders will be immortal" [4].

Notwithstanding the possibility that the sounds recorded on Thomas Edison's phonograph cylinders may indeed have, in a sense, become "immortal", as historic but most definitely non-supernatural artefacts, nonetheless Edison's opinion did not remain fixed throughout his life. *The American Magazine* of October 1920 reported firstly that the then 73-year-old Edison had changed his mind about belief in life-after-death, and secondly that Edison claimed to be developing (what was later referred to as) a "psychic telephone" [5] for actively making contact with the deceased [6]. In a later *Scientific American* article Edison stated that if, after death, "our personality survives, then it is strictly logical or scientific to assume that it retains memory, intellect, and other faculties and knowledge that we acquire on this Earth". Edison went on to say that "if personality exists after what we call death, it's reasonable to conclude that those who leave the Earth would like to communicate with those they have left here", and to assert that because he believed that "our personality hereafter will be able to affect matter", therefore "if we can evolve an instrument so delicate as to be affected, or moved, or manipulated by our personality as it survives in the next life, such an instrument, when made available, ought to record something" [7][8][9][10].

Repeated use of the word "if", and the question of whether it could ever be "strictly logical" to "assume" anything without hard evidence, all suggest Edison's reasoning might have been somewhat less than completely faultless, but nonetheless, with such support, Spiritualist beliefs progressed from a situation in which they'd survived their own movement's founders admitting they'd faked their evidence, to a situation in which they were instead receiving support from one of the world's most famous scientists. In Edison's case his change of heart may come as less of a surprise when we factor-in the additional influence that, as writer Eric Kluitenberg observes, Edison's parents were Spiritualists and that Edison's later statements may in part have been motivated by a commercial need to keep on generating sensational headline-grabbing publicity [11]. Martin Gardner suggests that Edison may have been influenced by a desire to impress his second (much younger) wife Mina Miller, who was a strict Methodist and anti-evolutionist [12], and Kluitenberg and Gardner both point out that despite his reputation as a great scientist, Edison pursued a life-long fascination with Theosophy and occultism, and that he was passionate in his defence of psychokinesis and extra-sensory perception demonstrations given by the stage magician Bert Reese. Finally, most importantly, Gardner also details numerous examples of how Edison made other predictions and statements about the future of science and technology which ultimately turned out to be *wrong* – including statements that "the talking motion picture will not supplant the regular silent motion picture" (*Munsey's Magazine*, March 1913), "it is apparent to me that the possibilities of the aeroplane... have been exhausted" (New York World, November 1895), "the radio craze... will die out in time so far as music is concerned" [13], and "the phonograph... is not of any commercial value" [14].

Although the credibility of Spiritualism had also suffered from active debunking by the great scientist and devout Christian Michael Faraday (1791-1867) and by the stage-magician and escapologist Harry Houdini (1874-1926), Edison's speculations were echoed in beliefs that were surprisingly common among some distinguished scientists of the late Victorian period and early 20th century. The chemist and physicist Sir William Crookes (1832-1919) invented the luminous Crookes Tube and spinthariscope, and was an enthusiastic supporter of the theory of "luminiferous aether", which posited the existence of a ubiquitous hypothetical substance which Crookes believed provided a medium for the transmission not only of light and Hertzian (radio) waves, but also for the transmission of human consciousness after death. The existence of ether was conclusively disproved by physicists Albert Michelson and Edward Morley in 1887, in experiments for which Michelson received the Nobel Prize and which paved the way for Einstein's Theory of Relativity; however, despite this, the physicist and radio pioneer Sir Oliver Lodge (1851-1940) wrote *Ether and Reality* as late as 1925, stating that "thought is not proven to be a secretion of the brain" [15] and concluding that ether "is the primary instrument of Mind, the vehicle of Soul, the habitation of Spirit... (and) the living garment of God" [16]. Although *Ether and Reality* only supported the possibility of communicating with the dead by implication, the human tragedy which underpinned Lodge's faith in this by then disproven theory was only too apparent, as, devastated by the death of his son in WW1, Lodge had written *Raymond, or Life and Death* in 1916 [17], and the book became a best-seller. Spiritualist beliefs also received an influential "celebrity endorsement" from Lodge's fellow Ghost Club member – Sherlock Holmes author Sir Arthur Conan Doyle, whose wife, brother, two brothers-in-law and beloved son Kingsley had all passed away either before or during WW1.

A good example that bears testament to the level of public interest in what would later evolve into and become known as EVP, is the discussion of "Psychic Phenomena and Wireless" written by PJ Risdon (FRSA) for the

August 1922 edition of *Popular Wireless Weekly*. Risdon's article offered a predictably "impartial" and "scientific" perspective on the belief that radio "may possibly assist in effecting communication with the spirit world", but remained circumspect, concluding that there was (at that time) "no present means of judging as to whether electromagnetic waves would constitute the means of such communications" [18]. The perception, promoted by Thomas Edison, William Crookes, Oliver Lodge and Arthur Conan Doyle etc, that the reality of life-after-death might eventually be established by scientific means, proved to have an enduring legacy, strongly influencing post-war developments in Spiritualist thought. However the "means" referred to by Risdon was not provided until its discovery by EVP researchers after WW2; and while we'll examine the subject of EVP specifically in more detail later, Edison's statement that "an instrument... affected... by our personality as it survives in the next life... ought to record something" continues to be cited as evidence of the alleged scientific respectability of EVP research to this day. Indeed a paraphrased version of Edison's statement appears as the opening sequence in the Hollywood movie *White Noise*, immediately followed by a dictionary-style definition of the term EVP, which categorically states that "voices and images of the dead..." are "now the subject of increasing scientific research" [19]; and while *White Noise* depicts EVP research for the purposes of entertainment, in context of a self-evidently fictional narrative, nonetheless this film strongly encourages its (large) audiences to think of EVP research as being truly scientific, not only by foregrounding such opening statements, but also because the film's DVD release includes several "factual" documentaries as special features, all of which present EVP recording as serious research. In the documentary *Hearing is Believing* for instance, AA-EVP research group director Lisa Butler contextualises the narrative of the main feature by categorically stating that EVP recordings are "objective evidence" [20].

Evidence of a link between some of the more speculative statements of the interwar period, and the more forthright language that we'll see later adopted by post-war EVP researchers, was provided by the publication in 1931 of *On the Edge of the Etheric, or Survival after Death, Scientifically Explained*, a book written by Glaswegian stock-broker and Spiritualist Arthur Findlay [21]. In terms of virtually shouting from his own front cover that Findlay's work was "revolutionising the scientific and religious thought of Great Britain", and that "this book marks the entrance to..." nothing short of "a new age of thought", from a contemporary perspective the sheer exuberance of this book's claims makes for amusing reading. Despite the extraordinary self-confidence of these pronouncements, *On the Edge* quotes a *Leicester Evening Mail* review as reporting that "this book is written in such *restrained language*..." (emphasis added) "and is so fascinating, that it should not be ignored by any genuine inquirer after truth".

On the Edge is however of interest as much for documenting its own public reception as it is for its (so-to-speak) "ideological" content, and if its language seems outlandish when read from the perspective of the early

21st century, it's sobering to note that between 1931 and 1951 Findlay's book claims to have sold-out no fewer than 49 separate printings. The 49th edition quotes 55 mainstream newspapers and periodicals (from *The Times* and *Glasgow Herald* to *The Investors Chronicle*) which gave positive reviews, and 15 similar recommendations from the Spiritualist and religious press (from *The National Spiritualist* to *The Occult Review*). The book received endorsements from the deputy governor of Northern Ireland, an ex-moderator of The Church of Scotland and from Oliver Lodge, was printed in Braille and translated into 18 languages (including the native languages of post-war EVP researchers Konstantin Raudive and Friedrich Jürgenson, of whom we'll learn more later). Mediumship is absolutely forbidden by mainstream Christian theology – The Book of Leviticus states that "a man or a woman who is a medium or a necromancer shall surely be put to death" (Leviticus 20:27, see also Deuteronomy 18:10-13), and this may explain why reviews in *The Daily Express* and *Wolverhampton Express & Star* referred to an official publication of The Church of Scotland refusing to accept advertisements for Findlay's book, and of its being banned "in certain church circles". However, as the *Evening Standard* added, "it is a truism that to have a book banned is the surest way to fly its banner before the public gaze". *The Wolverhampton Express* also discussed Findlay's investigations into "Direct Voice Phenomena", which may well shed light the origin of the later term Electronic Voice Phenomena [22].

In the book's foreword, Arthur Findlay gives a clear

indication of the sheer scale of his authorial ambitions, confirming that his purpose in writing the book was to "lay the foundations for Spiritualism becoming accepted as *the* religion, *the* science, and *the* philosophy of mankind" [23] (emphases added). Findlay's book contains a diagram, entitled "Visible and Invisible Vibrations", which encapsulates his underlying concept. The diagram depicts the electromagnetic spectrum – from what it calls Long Radio Waves, Micro Waves, Short Radio Waves and Heat Waves, through the Physical World (depicted in black, and corresponding to visible light) and the Etheric World, then to Soft X Rays, X Rays and Gamma Rays, stating that above and below this continuum lies the Unknown (no jokes about dragons, please) [24]. The section towards the centre of the spectrum is described as the Physical World, despite *all* phenomena within the spectrum being self-evidently physical, and the microwave and shortwave sections are depicted in the wrong order. The diagram's legend states that "the above chart makes clear how limited are our sense perceptions (as) only the black portion represents the visible spectrum", despite the fact that radio science and X-ray photography make phenomena from large parts of this spectrum accessible to human perception. The legend also states that "the author has been told by his informants in the Etheric World that its vibrations... can be detected by clairvoyance, by the seeing of etheric beings, called ghosts, and by psychic photography".

As to the nature of Findlay's own experiences of communicating with the afterlife however, he describes "strange and wonderful" contacts, experienced from September 1918 onwards, in the company of "the most gifted medium" John Sloan, in which "voices quite extraneous to the medium spoke to me, claiming to be those friends who, in my ignorance, I had looked upon as dead" [25]. As mentioned, anticipating the language of EVP, this speech is referred to as "Direct or Independent Voice... the highest psychical phenomena yet discovered", as "all the other discoveries of man fade into insignificance when compared to this great discovery" [26]. These séances encouraged Findlay to believe in what he referred to as "the science of Psychics", through whose development the previously opposing cultures of science and religion "will go hand-in-hand, brought together by the discoveries made by those who have devoted their lives to the furtherance of the knowledge gained by psychical research" [27]. With regard to relationships between the cultures of not religion, but of *art* and science, and with respect to what this present chapter will go on to say about the interest shown in Spiritualism by some contemporary artists, it is interesting to note that other individuals acknowledged by Findlay for their alleged enthusiasm for psychic research are the poet "Lord Tennyson (and) Watts and Leighton the painters" – so, on a point of detail, there also seems to be nothing new about artists being interested in Spiritualism [28].

Returning to Arthur Findlay's descriptions of ghost voices themselves, at the first séance attended by Findlay in 1918, John Sloan overcame the author's initial scepticism, as, over several hours, "thirty separate voices spoke", using "different tone and accent" to discuss accurate personal details with an audience of 15 people. While acknowledging that, if faked, such an effect would have required skilled performers, Findlay's testimony does little to disprove the obvious assumption that the medium might just have been, or have employed, one or more talented ventriloquists, especially since Findlay conceded that the séance took place in darkness (darkness which Findlay counterintuitively asserts "really increased the evidence in favour of the genuineness of the whole proceedings"). Even more strangely, even though Findlay conceded that "the balance was certainly in favour of fraud", he then went on to become convinced that these voices were supernatural, when two voices addressed him, discussing facts of which he was "the only living person with any knowledge", one being the voice of his father. If however we consider another obvious possibility, that these voices may have been produced by Findlay's own mind, it goes without saying that his mind would have been well aware of facts of which only he had knowledge [29].

Although Spiritualism as a movement and as a belief system attracted many followers, and although the publicity generated by for example Thomas Edison's claims seems to have been substantial, for many years Spiritualism remained focussed on the very tangibly human voices of actual clairvoyants and psychic mediums, such as those described by Arthur Findlay, and investigations into technologically mediated spirit communications of the sort predicted by *Popular Wireless* do not seem to have taken off until the latter part of the 20th century.

While it was certainly possible to make audio recordings of séances before then, using for instance wax cylinder recorders, with one notable exception, there seems to be no record of "etheric" (electromagnetic) means being used to materialise discarnate voices, until the machine which ghosts eventually chose to haunt later materialised, after WW2, in the form of the first commercially available magnetic tape recorders.

In fact magnetic tape recorders were preceded by more primitive (and much rarer) steel wire recorders, and the exception referred to above is that, when interviewed for a Channel 4 TV documentary called *Witness: Voices of the Dead* broadcast in 2001, a Catholic priest, theology professor and EVP author called François Brune claimed that EVP had in fact been recorded as early as 1952. According to Brune's description, one Father Ernetti and Papal chief scientist Father Gemelli were recording Gregorian chant at the Catholic University in Milan, when the wire snapped, and in frustration Father Gemelli cried out "oh father, help me". On playing back the repaired spool of wire Gemelli heard the sound of his own father replying "of course I'm helping you, I am always with you". This recording was then allegedly played-back to Pope Pius XII, who is said to have responded by stating that this contact was not sacrilegious, because in this case it was the dead who had contacted the living, without the intercession of a medium, and not the other way round. This incident did not yet signal the birth of the EVP movement as a social phenomenon however, because, according to François Brune "this experiment however was not published" [30].

The Catholic University incident notwithstanding, following the earlier precedents, the contemporary Electronic Voice Phenomena movement began in earnest after 1957, when Friedrich Jürgenson (1903-1987), a Swedish painter who executed portrait commissions for Pope Pius XII and Pope Paul VI, found human voices intruding onto tape recordings he'd made of his own voice and then, in 1959, of birdsong [31]. Convinced that these recorded sounds represented communications from aliens and later from his deceased mother, Jürgenson temporarily abandoned his artistic career to concentrate on these experiments, and to publicise his belief that his tapes constituted hard evidence proving the existence of the afterlife. In 1960 Jürgenson started recording similar tapes using radio equipment, and authored the books *Rösterna Från Rymden* (The Voices from Space) [32], *Sprechfunk Mit Verstorbenen* (Voice Transmissions With The Deceased) [33], and *Radio och Mikrofonkontakt med de Döda* (Radio and Microphone Contact with the Dead) [34].

As described in some detail in my own earlier publications [35], what Jürgenson had stumbled upon was the tendency of radios, tape recorders, microphones and even simply audio amplifiers, to (from time-to-time) pick-up so-called "stray" voice transmissions, usually from taxi and delivery firms, police and emergency services, passing aircraft, and in some locations maritime radio and even military exercises etc. Radio voice transmission and reception can be a surprisingly messy and inexact science, and it's a simple fact that electronic audio devices can, and often do, pick-up fragments of unwanted speech and other signals. When they are heard, stray voices can be extremely quiet, distorted and abrupt, are often shrouded in electrical interference and atmospheric noise, and my publications detail a battery of anecdotal reports and formal psychoacoustics experiments which show how the mind imposes illusory and subjective meaning onto such ambiguous sounds, in much the same way that viewers project meaning onto the random visual forms of psychoanalysts' famous Rorschach inkblot tests. Common-or-garden manifestations of such misperceptions are so well-known as to have been parodied in the TV adverts which presented misheard lyrics to Desmond Dekker's song *The Israelites* as "me ears are alight" and the slogan "compare the market" as "compare the meerkat", and a character in the cartoon Madagascar mishears "Grand Central Station" as "my aunt's constipation", etc (and the "discoveries" of EVP researchers are no more profound than that). Although the use of Rorschach tests is no longer common in psychoanalysis, I am confident most readers will be aware of the process whereby analysts asked clients to report what images they "see" in symmetrical splashes of ink; and, as with Rorschach tests, my articles argued that illusions of sound may, by a similar process, also reveal something of the listeners' own minds. Psychoacoustics experiments show firstly how listeners are much more susceptible to perceiving audio illusions when ambiguous sounds are played to them over and over again, as is standard practice with EVP, secondly how EVP researchers use prompting to convince listeners that sounds have been interpreted in "objective" (ie – shared) ways, and thirdly how listeners are more likely to project meanings they've been prompted to "hear" when speech is obscured by deliberately adding noise – another technique that is used by EVP researchers to (paradoxically) increase success in recording EVP. Projecting effects are in fact fundamental to normal audio perception and also to visual perception, even more so when (as is the case with EVP) combined with and amplified by emotions as powerful as those that accompany bereavement. As described by *The Oxford Companion to the Mind*, "in most bereaved people the urge to search for the lost person is reflected in thoughts, actions and perceptions...", and, in light of the bereavements suffered by many EVP enthusiasts, it is particularly interesting that "sights and *sounds* are commonly misperceived as evidence of his or her return" [36] (emphasis added).

Alongside the wealth of information provided by formal psychological studies, my articles also presented the example of the radio voices in Jean Cocteau's film *Orphée* (1950) [37] as anecdotal evidence of how it is that, as is often reported by EVP enthusiasts, radio voices can be misperceived as speaking to listeners directly and *personally*. During the film, the character of the poet Orpheus is shown receiving messages from the metaphysical Underworld, in the form of mysterious voices which he hears on the car radio of his Rolls Royce Silver

Ghost. Although the story depicted in *Orphée* is absolutely fictional, the film achieved the magnetic intensity of its brooding atmospheres by echoing experiences that haunted French society as it emerged from the shadow of Nazi occupation – one of those experiences being how French radio listeners reacted to hearing coded broadcasts sent by the BBC to the French resistance during WW2. "Silence is twice as fast backwards, three times" and "one glass of water illumines the world, twice" are examples from Cocteau's sound design which were stylistically modelled on coded broadcasts sent to the French Maquis by the British. Orpheus asks Heurtebise, "Where could they be coming from? No other station broadcasts them. I feel certain they are addressed to me personally" [38].

Like Jean Cocteau's fictional character Orpheus, Friedrich Jürgenson also believed that his radio voices spoke to him personally, his publications describing this attracted considerable attention, and, although it has since been claimed by his defenders that this reward was "due to his making of religious films, rather than (for) his work on EVP" [39], Jürgenson was awarded a Papal Knighthood by Pope Paul VI. The question here is in other words about whether Jürgenson was encouraged in his EVP work by the Vatican. Jürgenson's research also attracted the attention of a former student of Carl Jung, a Latvian psychologist and fellow Roman Catholic named Konstantin Raudive (1909-1974). Raudive visited Jürgenson in April 1965 [40], and took up the cause of EVP research, eventually (it is often said) building-up an archive of tens of thousands of magnetic tape recordings. Having been "greatly affected" by the death of his friend Margarete Petrautzki [41], the bereaved Raudive visited Jürgenson for a second time in June 1965, and dedicated himself to EVP research. By 1968 Raudive had accumulated sufficient evidence to be able to document his findings in the first version of his book *Unhörbares Wird Hörbar* (The Inaudible Becomes Audible) [42] – whose translation was published in 1971 as *Breakthrough*. With a level of confidence equivalent to that shown by Arthur Findlay, *Breakthrough* proclaimed EVP research to readers as "of unquestionable importance", as "amazing", as "revolutionary", and as an "astounding scientific phenomenon".

Konstantin Raudive successfully marketed *Breakthrough* to its English language publisher at the Frankfurt Bookfair in 1969 [43], and, largely on account of his book's availability in English, EVP research is as a result arguably better known through the work of Raudive than through the work of his predecessor Friedrich Jürgenson. However, the overwhelming majority of individuals who have come across Raudive's work seem to have done so as a result of hearing snippets from his recorded tapes – at least some of which have been deposited in the Sound Archive of the British Library [44] – and from coming across references to his work in newspapers and magazines and on TV and in movies. The *Breakthrough* book itself does not seem to have been very widely read or quoted, but still appears to be regarded by most EVP enthusiasts as effectively the definitive and classic text of EVP research. As such Raudive's book rewards more detailed attention, not least because readers get a strong impression of the nature and scope of its author's intentions immediately they read even the first paragraph. From the opening page of *Breakthrough* we learn that "the explorer" (or EVP researcher) has both an "adventurous spirit" but also "deep humility", however by page 12 we get a less disingenuous sense of the significance that Raudive attached to his work, when we learn that in fact the importance of the "voice phenomenon is equal to nuclear physics".

While at first glance the hardback edition of *Breakthrough* does look sufficiently impressive to do at least superficial justice to such grandiose aspirations, in terms of critical and technical analysis Raudive's discourse turns out to be remarkably sparse. *Breakthrough* contains a 20-page preface by Peter Bander, describing how the publisher Colin Smythe was persuaded to take up Raudive's book, and detailing Bander's experiences of EVP recording. This preface is followed by Raudive's first 33-page chapter and by 268 pages of transcribed voice recordings. Scattered notes within those transcripts notwithstanding, the transcripts are followed by just five pages of conclusion, and by 85 pages of "expert" third party commentary contained in the book's Appendices. In this way, despite the book's near 400-page bulk, Raudive's own substantive discourse – the introduction and conclusions in which he argues his case for the seriousness and validity of his research – adds up to a somewhat less impressive 38 pages.

Anticipating (and no doubt strongly influencing) Lisa Butler's later statement that EVP recordings are "objective evidence", and having repeatedly claimed that his research was "scientific", Raudive also stated that the "tape recorder, radio and microphone give us facts in an entirely impersonal way, and their objectivity cannot be challenged" [45]. Similarly Jenny Randles states in her book *The Unexplained* that EVP recordings are "technological proof of life after death" [46], also echoing the assertion made by François Brune, that when the broken wire recording was played to Pius XII, the Pope stated that "a recorder is objective", and that (despite the theological truism that real faith does not require evidence) "this could be the beginning of a scientific discovery who could help to the faith in the eternal life" [47]. Such statements all point to another interesting fact, which is that one of the reasons EVP enthusiasts allow themselves to interpret audio illusions as scientifically objective evidence, is because these illusions of sound are, in the believer's perception, mutually supported by an equivalent visual illusion. The illusion in question is that, in making use of technological products of scientific research – tape recorders, radios, microphones, also often oscilloscopes and more recently digital recording devices and computers etc – EVP research set-ups superficially resemble scientific experiments (and of course illusions like this do convince people, because TV advertisers use illusions of science to sell products all the time). Hard science exists however as much in the domain of the chalk board, the back-of-the-envelope calculation and the thought-experiment, as it exists in the world of electrical machinery, issues of how experiments are carried out are just as important as any technology that's used to conduct them, and EVP researchers seem, from Raudive onwards, to be almost totally ignorant of anything remotely resembling philosophy of science or scientific methodology. Despite, and in some ways because of, the use of electronic, laboratory and communications technology, EVP research is in fact far closer to conjuring tricks and to stage magic than it is to genuinely scientific research.

Raudive thought he heard his mother address him by his nicknames "Kosti" and "Kostulit" [48], and heard voices of other deceased friends and relatives – an auntie who had become a nun [49], his sister Tekle [50] and friends Aljosha, Sonja and Aileen [51], among many others. Jürgenson heard his mother personally address him over dead frequencies using his childhood nickname "Friedl"; and, with regard to research methodology, Raudive states that of the "roughly 72,000 audible voices" that he claimed to have archived, it was "the mother-motive (that) is statistically the most frequent" [52]. Raudive further suggests that he analysed approximately 25,000 of his 72,000 recordings, but, beyond citing these two figures, and unlike most genuinely scientific research, in fact no "statistical" or even basic numerical analyses seem to have been presented anywhere else in *Breakthrough*. It would be hard not to empathise however, because the impression one retains most vividly from reading Raudive's book is not so much one of poor methodology, but instead the impression of profound grief.

While attempts have been made to link EVP as

a cultural phenomenon to the Cold War, in fact the EVP movement had strong precedents before that and continues to outlive the Cold War to this day. It was not until 18 years after the Cold War began (in 1946) that Jürgenson published his first book (in 1964), and while Raudive's *Breakthrough* was published during the Cold War (in 1971), his work was most profoundly influenced by preceding events. Indeed, Raudive was so traumatised by experiences of WW2 that four pages of his book are dedicated to detailing dozens of contacts with Adolf Hitler and Benito Mussolini [53]. Similarly, according to sleevenotes of the *Friedrich Jürgenson – From the Studio for Audioscopic Research* CD [54], Jürgensen recorded contacts with Adolf Hitler, the Theosophist Annie Besant, Sir Oliver Lodge, Albert Einstein, Hilde Goebbels, and Felix Kersten – an "old friend of Jürgensen" who'd been Heinrich Himmler's masseur (and who claimed to have used that relationship to save tens of thousands of people from murder by the Nazis). While there is no doubt that Raudive accused Hitler of "spiritual depravity", we also learn he'd recorded voices he attributed to his deceased employee Margarete Petrautzki, who it transpires had previously been employed by the Hitler Youth [55]. In fact Raudive states that EVP recordings "by Hitler or about him could fill a separate book" [56].

One of several paradoxes of EVP is that enthusiasts tend to believe in the illusion that EVP research is "scientific" at least partly because they know that the evidence they present in support of their claims is (often, if not always) genuinely real, and because the observations that they report are descriptions of that which in many cases they really have recorded. Konstantin Raudive was himself a classic example of those EVP enthusiasts who prefer to assume that scientifically-minded critics of EVP would dismiss his discoveries as fantasies, in contrast to the "objective" reality of the hard evidence that EVP researchers really do record on tape. What is missing from such analysis is however any real understanding of how psychoacoustic processes enable listeners to totally misinterpret that evidence, and any understanding of how the application of genuinely scientific research methods would help inure researchers against falling prey to such self-deceptions.

According to the *Witness* TV documentary "today more than 30,000 believers in 87 countries belong to EVP societies", but one of the strangest manifestations of this movement's popularity is the degree of support which EVP seems to enjoy within sections of the fine-arts community, including many sound artists, electronic musicians and installation artists, who have used EVP material in their work. A good deal of this support seems to have at least partly arisen as a side-effect of the interest shown in EVP by the writer William Burroughs. Burroughs was himself also a practicing sound artist, often working with human voices recorded on magnetic tape. It would be an understatement to say that his influence on avant-garde, fine-arts and electronic music cultures has been enormous, and anecdotally I can report that many EVP apologists within the arts defer to Burroughs when rationalising their support for EVP. More concretely, a

CD called *Konstantin Raudive – The Voices of the Dead* (which features Raudive tapes remixed by a number of prominent sound artists) was published by Sub Rosa (a Belgian record company notable for issuing tribute CDs to the postmodernist philosopher Gilles Deleuze). The CD sleevenotes confirm that "for many the first traces of the Raudive taped experiments were found in William Burroughs's works of fiction", and assert that "the fact is, these mysterious magnetic tapes... which were recorded by the Baltic scientist Konstantin Raudive, are not fiction but reality". The commentary goes on to state that "we are not here to judge their scientific objectivity", but then effectively does so anyway, by stating that EVP is "a classic issue of perception... a question as old as time itself – the shape of clouds, divination, auspices to be able to read entrails, blood or the air for things to come" [57], and explains that Burroughs' relationship with Raudive's work was central to the concept underpinning this CD.

As to what Burroughs definitely got right, in an essay entitled *Les Voleurs* the link between literature and sound art is established by a truism that seems obvious to almost everyone except most people involved in mainstream contemporary art - namely his statement that "writers work with words and voices just as painters work with colours" [58]. As a result it's not surprising that Burroughs explored the use of magnetic tape to manipulate sounds of words and voices for literary effect. To paraphrase Aristotle's *Poetics*, written language is based on symbolic visual representations of indivisible *sounds* [59] - therefore firstly (as I've previously written) all literature and poetry are forms of sound art [60], and secondly the earliest form of sound recording technology was not a machine but was *written language*.

In the opening paragraph of his essay *It Belongs to the Cucumbers* (whose title is a quote from Raudive), Burroughs stated that *Breakthrough* is "the most complete source book" on EVP [61], and went on to describe voice manipulation experiments which he conducted with the artist Brion Gysin some time after 1959. "We went on to exploit the potentials of the tape recorder: cut up, slow down, speed up, run backwards, inch the tape, play several tracks at once, cut back and forth between two recorders", and, as a result "you will get new words that were not on the original recordings" [62]. Indeed Burroughs implied a working knowledge of psychoacoustic projection when he described how "I have gotten words and voices from (recordings of) barking dogs", and that "words will emerge from recordings of dripping faucets... in fact, almost any sound that is not too uniform may produce words". Burroughs went on to quote a song (recorded by Maurice Chevalier) that says "every little breeze seems to whisper Louise", adding his own line that says "the very tree branches brushing against her window seemed to mutter *murder, murder, murder*". Echoing Jürgenson, Raudive and Cocteau, Burroughs then described how "some time ago a young man came to see me and said he was going mad" because "street signs, overheard conversations, radio broadcasts, seemed to refer to him in some way" [63], and Burroughs recalled a friend who went "mad" (the inverted commas are Burroughs' originals) after hearing "personal messages from Arab broadcasts" [64].

William Burroughs believed however that tape recording machines functioned in a way that resembles human memory, asking readers to "remember that your memory bank contains tapes of everything that you have ever heard... press a button, and a news broadcast you heard 10 years ago plays back". Even if accurate, this observation is at best banal, as all mechanisms that record experiences also recall or elicit *memories* of experiences, but the sound-art theorist and historian Douglas Kahn [65] contends that Burroughs' interest in this analogy was influenced by Church of Scientology founder and sci-fi writer L Ron Hubbard, and Burroughs confirms that in 1968 he studied at a Scientology centre in England [66].

William Burroughs was certainly no uncritical fan of Raudive, pointing out logical inconsistencies in Raudive's reasoning, but according to Douglas Kahn, the reason Burroughs "championed Raudive voices" was because he felt that EVP recordings "prove the case against the whole psychiatric dogma that (the) voices are the imaginings of a sick mind". Burroughs felt this perceived dogma had been "called into question" because, echoing the statements of many EVP believers, the voices "are of extraneous origin and are objectively and demonstrably there on tape..." although no-one ever disputed the voices were there on tape. In that way, Burroughs failed to understand the relevance of his own observations about how listening to "almost any sound that is not too uniform may produce words". So, in the sense that all people share a perfectly natural ability to perceive illusory words in ambiguous voice and sound recordings, Burroughs would (if this was his intention) have been right to believe that people are not mad simply because they hear illusory voices. It would however be disingenuous to somehow blame "psychiatric dogma" for his own friends reporting that they themselves *feared* their own mishearings might be either symptomatic of madness or might be driving them mad; but, then again, Burroughs was famous for his invocation to "Destroy All Rational Thought".

Where madness might come into play however is (fortunately) not in our capacity for mishearing itself, but (unfortunately) in the extreme significance that a minority of listeners might misattribute to specific examples of mishearing. There are also chicken-and-egg arguments as to the mental states of people who attribute great significance to misheard sounds, as it would be irresponsible not to concede that emotional and psychiatric issues could be aggravated, or in extreme cases even produced, by obsessive fixation on "evidence" that's interpreted as completely overturning conventional notions of reality. As a case in point, where William Burroughs reported hearing human voices in recordings of dogs, EVP obsessive and music impresario Joe Meek – the producer of *Johnny Remember Me* – heard human voices in cat meowing that he'd recorded in a graveyard, and it's an open question whether Meek's obsession with the occult may have contributed to the breakdown which led him to kill his landlady and then shoot himself [67].

According to the sleevenotes of the *Audioscopic Research* CD, Jürgenson described "a message about a central investigation station in space, from where they conducted profound observations of mankind", stating that "my friends spoke about certain electromagnetic screens or radars, that were frequently transmitted, day and night, in thousands to our three dimensional life levels and like living beings had a mission as mental messengers. Undoubtedly one could see these radars as half living robots that, remote controlled, had the ability like an oversensitive television or radio to correctly register and transmit all our conscious and unconscious impulses, feelings and thoughts". To be fair, the garbled nature of that passage might to some extent be attributable to poor translation, but statements about how TV and radio might "register and transmit all our conscious and unconscious impulses, feelings and thoughts" would concern readers with even a slight knowledge of clinical psychiatry, as will the fact that Jürgenson also described these messages as being received by "telepathic" means. Jürgenson didn't think he was mad however, he thought "these events were produced by his highly developed aural and visual senses caused by his artistic prowess".

While acknowledging that psychiatry and psychoanalysis aren't exactly the same thing, nonetheless, given William Burroughs' antipathy to interpreting mishearings as to what he projected as being "psychiatric dogma", it seems appropriate to offer the floor here to the father of psychoanalysis. It is consistent with the view that EVP as a *religious belief system* stems from the misunderstanding of audio illusions, that Sigmund Freud bluntly stated in his book *The Future of an Illusion* that "the psychical origin of religious ideas" does not stem from "experience or (from the) end-results of thinking", but that it stems from "illusions, fulfillments of the oldest, strongest and most urgent wishes of mankind" [68]. Given the beliefs of Lodge and Findlay etc, it also seems appropriate that Freud observed how, for those who believe in it, life after death "continues life on earth just as the invisible part of the spectrum joins onto the visible part" [69]. As for the question of madness, Freud's actual view runs contrary to the assumption made by Burroughs, stating that "devout believers are safeguarded... against the risk of certain neurotic illnesses", because "their acceptance of the universal neurosis..." (their acceptance of a religious belief system) "spares them the task of constructing a personal one" [70]. As to the question of integrity however, Freud asserts that "where questions of religion are concerned, people are guilty of every possible sort of dishonesty and intellectual misdemeanour" [71], and his observation was not intended to be taken as just a generalisation, as Freud comments specifically on Spiritualism...

"If all the evidence put forward for the authenticity of religious teachings originates in the past, it is natural to look round and see whether the present... may not also be able to furnish evidence... The proceedings of the spiritualists meet us at this point; they are convinced of the survival of the individual soul, and they seek to demonstrate to us beyond doubt the truth of this one religious doctrine. Unfortunately they cannot succeed in refuting the fact that the appearance and utterances of their spirits are merely the products of their own mental activity. They have called up the spirits of the greatest men and the most eminent thinkers, but all the pronouncements and information which they have received from them have been so foolish and so wretchedly meaningless that one can find nothing in them but the capacity of the spirits to adapt themselves to the circle of people who have conjured them up" [72].

As to the ethical dilemma of disillusioning people of belief in life after death, Freud asserts that "those who do not suffer from the neurosis will need no intoxicant to deaden it", and that although people will therefore "have to admit... the full extent of their insignificance in the machinery of the universe", in regard to "education to reality" he believed that "men cannot remain children forever" [73]. Again as regards the question of integrity, it is appropriate that what amounts to the last word on Konstantin Raudive's research was provided by Raudive's... last word – the posthumous publication, the year after his death, of *Der Fall Wellensittich* (The Case of the Budgerigar) [74]. Very little information is available about this book in English, but there's plenty in German (and at the time of writing it can be purchased via Amazon for 0.01 Euros). According to sound art curator David Briers, Raudive's final investigation concerned cassette tapes of a budgie called Putzi, who was "alleged to have functioned as a mediumistic channel for its deceased owner" [75].

The *Rorschach Audio* concept takes as its central metaphor the idea that, as a contemporary manifestation of Spiritualism, EVP is a religious belief system based on the misperception of illusions of sound. In comparison, in his book *Language, Truth & Logic*, the humanist philosopher AJ Ayer put forward the view that all metaphysical and religious statements are, from the point of view of factually verifiable truth, inherently and literally meaningless. While later admitting that his judgement in this respect had been "harsh" and that *Language, Truth & Logic* had been "a young man's book" [76] – tacitly acknowledging, in my interpretation, that as an older man he came to recognise how religious beliefs can have emotional as well as just factual meaning, nonetheless Ayer's book stated that in effect metaphysical philosophers are thinkers who have been "duped by grammar" [77], by the superficial appearance of certain statements, into perceiving in those statements what I would describe as illusions of meaning. So, although Freddie Ayer's writing did not explicitly and categorically identify metaphysical statements as illusions, using that exact terminology, nonetheless these statements are illusory, and in this way Ayer's argument pointed to what amounts to the parallel existence of *illusions of language*.

In relation to ideas about *The Ghost in the Machine* introduced by the philosopher Gilbert Ryle [78] and popularised by Arthur Koestler [79] – ideas in which the "ghost" is taken to represent aspects of the human mind, and the "machine" is taken to represent the body – extrapolating and applying such terminology to literal (non-human) machines, it is also interesting to note that AJ Ayer proposed a test to establish whether any apparently conscious being really has a mind, or whether that being is a truly mechanical automaton. Ayer stated that "the only ground I can have for asserting that an object which appears to be conscious is not really a conscious being, but only a dummy or a machine, is that it fails to satisfy one of the empirical tests by which the presence or absence of consciousness is determined" [80]. Suggesting that the way to determine whether what appears to be a conscious being (say, for instance, a machine such as a robot or computer responding to its owner's questions) is really conscious or not, is to test for consciousness, may not at first seem particularly helpful, but Ayer's statement was a significant precursor to the notion of a Turing Test, which is one of the most important concepts in modern computer science. To summarise, the mathematician and cryptanalyst Alan Turing proposed that a machine could be said to have finally exhibited intelligent behaviour, if a human operator submitting questions through say a keyboard and workstation, could no longer distinguish between responses that were fed back from an unseen human operator and responses provided by an automated machine [81]. Ventriloquists are among the greatest artistic manipulators of audio illusions, and there is in this way a comparison to be made between the Turing Test and a ventriloquist's act. In the Turing Test the computer programmer seeks to demonstrate artificial intelligence by projecting the equivalent of his or her "voice" (their intelligence and their consciousness) onto their version of a ventriloquist's dummy (the user's workstation), sufficiently successfully that this machine's performance fools an audience into attributing human-like consciousness to that inanimate object. So, where in some contexts, the words "ghost" and "illusion" can be more-or-less synonymous (it's common for psychologists to refer to illusions as "perceptual ghosts" for instance), in context of how EVP researchers use machines to generate illusory evidence of discarnate consciousness, the words "ghost" and "consciousness" also become effectively synonymous, as articulations of an underlying (philosophically dualistic) assumption about the nature of human consciousness. Of course, there is nothing profound about simply demonstrating the fact that ghosts of the deceased are believed to have consciousness, but what is pertinent here is that such consciousness as EVP researchers appear to demonstrate in their recorded evidence is, by another equivalent of the ventriloquist's trick, their *own* consciousness. Similarly the intelligence displayed by the machines that Alan Turing spoke of building would indeed be *real* intelligence, but would belong to those machines' original programmers, and not to the machines – in both cases what these machines reveal is in fact an attribute of the people who made use of them.

With regard to such projective faculties, readers may well recall that, after the first wave of major publicity attracted by EVP, some Christian Evangelists campaigned against rock music on grounds of allegations that, when played backwards, particularly Heavy Metal albums contained "subliminal" Satanic messages. Without the space to go into too much detail here, these campaigns were pioneered by preachers Dan and Steve Peters of St. Paul, Minnesota, who founded the organisation Truth About Rock in 1979, and who attracted publicity throughout the 1980s with a series of high-profile TV interviews and public LP burnings. The method employed on Peters Brothers' demonstration cassettes consisted of taking snippets of sound from songs by The Beatles, ELO, Led Zeppelin, Queen and The Rolling Stones etc, and playing these sounds backwards, over and over, until the voices that emerged resembled words that echoed the Brothers' mind-sets. The similarity between their method and EVP research is hopefully self-evident, but one wonders why they even bothered to manufacture such evidence, since at least one member of Led Zeppelin was for instance an open devotee of the Satanist Aleister Crowley. A classic example of their method involved reversing the word "yes" (which appears, momentarily unaccompanied and most un-subliminally, in the track *You Took The Words Right Out Of My Mouth* by Meat Loaf) to create the sound "sey", onto which the Peters Brothers asked listeners to append the in fact totally non-existant sound "tan", in order to show how the offending track subliminally invoked music fans to worship "Satan". Risible as this may all sound, Truth About Rock was maintained as a successful business for many years, and pursued an overtly ideological right-wing agenda, which was, despite the Brothers' reassuringly informal and relaxed style of narration, explicitly homophobic and anti-humanist [82].

The most famous claim about this so-called Back-Masking was however that which resulted in a prosecution brought in 1990 against the rock group Judas Priest by James Vance, after he and fellow teenager Raymond Belknap shot themselves behind a church in Nevada, five years earlier in 1985, resulting in the extreme disfigurement of James Vance and the tragic death of Ray Belknap. The prosecution contended that the friends were encouraged to shoot themselves by the words "do it", which it was alleged were subliminally recorded into the Judas Priest song *Better By You, Better Than Me* [83]. Despite the obvious paradox that, even if these words had been hidden in the recording, the words "do it" still don't command listeners to do anything specific, least of all shoot themselves, nonetheless Judge Jerry Carr Whitehead agreed he did hear the alleged message, but concluded that this perception arose from accidental combinations of sounds rather than from the malicious placing of intentional messages. Although singer Rob Halford eventually admitted, under oath, that Judas Priest *did* place reversed messages in their songs, the case was thrown out after the band played reversed sections of their *Stained Class* LP to the court, to reveal equally convincing demonstrations of messages such as "hey ma, my chair's broken", "it's so fishy, personally I'll own it" and "I asked for a peppermint, I asked for her to get one" [84].

Controversies attending the politicisation of *Rorschach Audio* type phenomena have unfortunately not been confined to history however, as (for several years, and still at the time of writing) one only has to type the words "Obama is a" into a Google search window to see the depth of influence that smear-campaigns against

America's first black President have had on popular culture (notwithstanding the detail that, of course, Barack Obama is in fact mixed-heritage). The *Daily Mail* reported in August 2010 that "one in four Americans believe Obama is Muslim" [85], and, whether or not that figure is accurate, in context of Islamophobic campaigning around the perceived relationship between Muslims and terrorism, the political effect of such allegations is real, and there have been more than enough examples of US news anchors mishearing or misarticulating the word "Obama" as "Osama" (and vice-versa) to realise that this smear-campaign has benefitted from the ease with which these two sounds can be (accidentally or deliberately) confused. A classic example was US TV news presenter Geraldo Rivera stumbling to correct his report that "Obama is dead" shortly after the assassination of Osama Bin Laden. As an illustration of how projective mishearing can reveal the preoccupations and fears of not just individuals, but in fact of broader communities, it was also reported throughout international TV and print media in 2008 that outraged parents across the USA had objected to purchasing a talking Fisher Price "Little Mommy Cuddle & Coo" doll, whose automated blurbling of (roughly) "giglam igalite" was interpreted as saying "Islam is the Light" [86]. Obviously it's tempting to dismiss such nonsense for being what it is, but, as well as being simply quite funny, it's also sobering to note that, like Geraldo Rivera's comment, through being broadcast by Fox TV News, that audio illusion was potentially reported to an audience of over 100 million households.

[1] Richard Gregory (editor) *Oxford Companion to the Mind* Oxford University Press, 1987, p.293

[2] BE Carroll *Spiritualism in Antebellum America* Indiana University Press, Bloomington, 1997, p.248

[3] James Randi *An Encyclopedia of Claims, Frauds, and Hoaxes of the Occult and Supernatural* – http://www.randi.org/encyclopedia/encyclopedia.html#F – retrieved 27 Feb 2012

[4] Martin Gardner "Thomas Edison, Paranormalist" *Skeptical Inquirer* 1996

[5] Eric Kluitenberg *Connection Machines* Noemalab, Milan, 2005, p.8

[6] BC Forbes "Edison Working on How to Communicate with the Next World" *American Magazine*, 1920

[7] A Lescarboura "Edison's Views on Life after Death" *Scientific American*, 30 October 1920

[8] Pat Kubis & Mark Macy *Conversations Beyond the Light* Continuing Life Research, Boulder, 1995, p.100

[9] Eric Kluitenberg *Connection Machines* Noemalab, Milan, 2005, p.8

[10] Martin Gardner "Thomas Edison, Paranormalist" *Skeptical Inquirer* 1996

[11] Eric Kluitenberg *Connection Machines* Noemalab, Milan, 2005, p.8

[12] Martin Gardner "Thomas Edison, Paranormalist" *Skeptical Inquirer* 1996

[13] R Conot *A Streak of Luck* Seaview, New York, 1979, p.424

[14] R Conot, op.cit., 1979, p.245

[15] Oliver Lodge *Ether and Reality* Hodder & Stoughton, London, 1925, p.17
[16] Oliver Lodge, op.cit., p.179
[17] Oliver Lodge *Raymond, or Life and Death* Methuen, London, 1916
[18] PJ Risdon "Psychic Phenomena and Wireless" *Popular Wireless Weekly*, 1922, pp.237-238
[19] Geoffrey Sax (director) *White Noise* Gold Circle Films 2004
[20] Jim Moret (presenter) *Hearing is Believing* Universal Pictures 2005
[21] Arthur Findlay *On the Edge of the Etheric* Psychic Press, London, 1951
[22] Arthur Findlay, op.cit., pp.i-x
[23] Arthur Findlay, op.cit., p.7
[24] Arthur Findlay, op.cit., p.10
[25] Arthur Findlay, op.cit., p.12
[26] Arthur Findlay, op.cit., p.32
[27] Arthur Findlay, op.cit., p.21
[28] Arthur Findlay, op.cit., p.25
[29] Arthur Findlay, op.cit., pp.58-59
[30] David Monaghan (director) *Witness – Voices of the Dead* Channel 4 TV, 2001
[31] Mike Harding & C.M. von Hausswolff "1485.0 kHz" *Cabinet Magazine*, New York, Winter 2000, pp.56-61
[32] Friedrich Jürgenson *Rösterna Från Rymden* Saxon & Lindström, Stockholm, 1964
[33] Friedrich Jürgenson *Sprechfunk Mit Verstorbenen* Hermann Bauer KG, Freiburg, 1967
[34] Friedrich Jürgenson *Radio och Mikrofonkontakt med*

de Döda Nybloms, Uppsala, 1968

[35] Joe Banks "Rorschach Audio", sleevenotes in *The Ghost Orchid* CD, PARC / Ash International, 1999; "Rorschach Audio – A Lecture at The Royal Society of British Sculptors", *Diffusion* 8, Sonic Arts Network, August 2000, pp.2-6; "Rorschach Audio – Ghost Voices and Perceptual Creativity" *Leonardo Music Journal* vol.11, MIT Press, 2001, pp.77-83; "Rorschach Audio – Art and Illusion for Sound", *Strange Attractor Journal* vol.1, 2004, pp.124-159

[36] CM Parkes "Bereavement", quoted in RL Gregory, 1987. op.cit., p.80

[37] Jean Cocteau (writer/director) *Orphée* Andre Paulve Film & Films du Palais Royal, 1950

[38] Carol Martin-Sperry (translator) *Cocteau* Viking, New York, 1972, pp.101-191

[39] G Connelley *EVP – The Cinderella Science* Domra Publications, Corby, 2001, p.9

[40] Konstantin Raudive *Breakthrough* Colin Smythe, Gerrards Cross, 1971, p.14

[41] Konstantin Raudive, op.cit., p.15

[42] Konstantin Raudive *Unhörbares Wird Hörbar* Otto Reichl, Remagen, 1968

[43] Konstantin Raudive, op.cit., p.vii

[44] Toby Oakes "Recording the Paranormal" in *Playback – The Bulletin of the National Sound Archive*, 28, Winter 2002

[45] Konstantin Raudive, op.cit., p.1

[46] Jenny Randles *The Unexplained* Anaya 1994, p.87

[47] David Monaghan (director) *Witness – Voices of the*

Dead Channel 4 TV, 2001

[48] Konstantin Raudive, op.cit., pp.35-38 & 47

[49] Konstantin Raudive, op.cit., pp.39-40

[50] Konstantin Raudive, op.cit., pp.40-41

[51] Konstantin Raudive, op.cit., pp.41-45

[52] Konstantin Raudive, op.cit., p.35

[53] Konstantin Raudive, op.cit., pp.88-91

[54] *Friedrich Jürgenson – From the Studio for Audioscopic Research* CD, Ash International / Färgfabriken / PARC, 2000

[55] Konstantin Raudive, op.cit., p.215

[56] Konstantin Raudive, op.cit., p.88

[57] Guy Marc Hinant *Konstantin Raudive – The Voices of the Dead* CD sleevenotes, Sub Rosa SR66, 2002

[58] William Burroughs *The Adding Machine* Arcade, New York, 1986, p.19 (originally printed in *Crawdaddy* magazine 68, 1976)

[59] SH Butcher (translator) *The Poetics of Aristotle* Macmillan, London, 1920, pp.70-71

[60] Joe Banks "Sound Anthology" *Art Monthly*, October 2001, p.47

[61] William Burroughs *The Adding Machine* Arcade, New York, 1993, p.52

[62] William Burroughs, op.cit., p.53

[63] William Burroughs, op.cit., p.53

[64] William Burroughs, op.cit., p.54

[65] Douglas Kahn *Noise, Water, Meat: A History of Sound in the Arts* The MIT Press, 1999, pp.219-220

[66] William Burroughs, op.cit., p.17

[67] John Repsch *The Legendary Joe Meek – The Telstar*

Man Cherry Red Books, London, 2001
[68] Sigmund Freud *The Future of an Illusion* Vintage, London, 2001, p.30
[69] Sigmund Freud, op.cit., p.19
[70] Sigmund Freud, op.cit., p.44
[71] Sigmund Freud, op.cit., p.33
[72] Sigmund Freud, op.cit., pp.28-29
[73] Sigmund Freud, op.cit., p.49
[74] Konstantin Raudive *Der Fall Wellensittich* Otto Reichl, Remagen, 1975
[75] David Briers "Audible Babel" in Clare Charnley & Katrin Kivimaa (editors) *So Communication* Estonian Academy of Art, 2007
[76] AJ Ayer *Language, Truth & Logic* Penguin, Harmondsworth, 1983, p.7
[77] AJ Ayer, op.cit., p.61
[78] Gilbert Ryle *The Concept of Mind* University of Chicago Press, 1949
[79] Arthur Koestler *The Ghost in the Machine* Penguin, London 1967
[80] AJ Ayer, op.cit., pp.171-172
[81] Alan Turing "Computing Machinery and Intelligence" *Mind*, 59, 1950, pp.433-460
[82] Peters Brothers *Backwards Masking – How Subliminals Affect You* (audio cassette) Truth About Rock Ministries, St Paul, circa 1985
[83] David Van Taylor (director) *Dream Deceivers* KNPB Channel 5 Public Broadcasting, 1992
[84] Emma Barker (director) *Dancing with the Devil* TVF / Channel 4, 1991

[85] Daniel Bates "Now one in four Americans believe Obama is Muslim as Ground Zero mosque row intensifies", *Daily Mail*, 19 August 2010

[86] Matthew Moore "Talking Fisher-Price Doll Accused of Promoting Islam" *Daily Telegraph*, 13 Oct 2008; Caroline Alphonso "Does Little Mommy Cuddle coo Islam is the Light?" *Toronto Globe & Mail*, 8 Dec 2008; Virginia Wheeler "Fury over Islam is Light Doll" *The Sun*, date unknown; "Parents Outraged Over Baby Doll They Say Mumbles Pro-Islam Message" *Fox News*, 9 October 2008

Acknowledgements

This article is partly based on a presentation about "Rorschach Audio" phenomena and Satanic Back-Masking given by Joe Banks and Poulomi Desai in the "Subliminal" Festival at Beursschouwburg, Brussels, 19 January 2005 – special thanks to Poulomi, to Hans de Man and Foton Records. The Obama-Osama mishearing is the basis for the *Rorschach Audio – Projective Apperception Test* parody, commissioned by MUU Helsinki and published on volume 3 of the *MUU For Ears* CD series in 2010 – special thanks to Rita Leppiniemi.

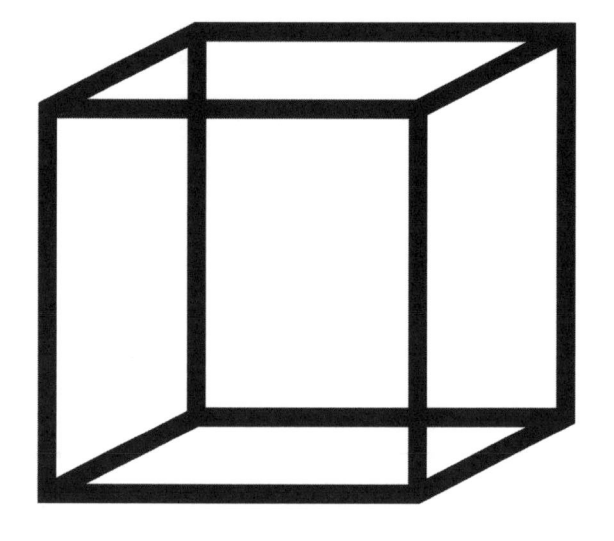

"L'Amour / La Mort"

Disinformation (after Jean Genet) © September 2011

Chapter 3
L'Amour / La Mort

"Jamaica? – No, she went of her own free will."
– PG Wodehouse *Uncle Dynamite* 1948

As readers of this book will by now hopefully be well aware, *Rorschach Audio* publications and lectures have been continually produced since 1999, up until now (and as summarised within the first chapter of this book) focussing primarily on the discussion of the Spiritualist so-called Electronic Voice Phenomena recordings. Extrapolating this earlier work, the purpose of this present chapter is to explore and to discuss relationships between *Rorschach Audio* type sound phenomena and artistic and literary creativity. To recap briefly, the earlier *Rorschach Audio* material argued that rather than their being either genuinely supernatural ghost voices, or purely figments of their authors' imaginations, EVP recordings are instead physically real material phenomena whose origin and nature EVP researchers have fundamentally misunderstood. The earlier publications argued that EVP recordings are the same "stray" radio voices that often demodulate onto electronic communications and recording equipment, and the public lectures that have accompanied this project use recordings of psychoacoustics experiments to enable audiences to personally experience how it is that the mind can and does actively project familiar meanings onto ambiguous sounds, imposing meaning in an equivalent way to how the mind projects images onto the random visual forms of Rorschach ink-blot tests. These presentations use a fair battery of anecdotal and experimental evidence to explain several apparently anomalous paradoxes associated with EVP listening, and, since many Spiritualists believe that the use of electronic recording technology makes EVP research "scientific", when in fact it is not, the *Rorschach Audio* presentations also argue a case for increased public understanding of mainstream scientific methodology, explaining why it is that EVP experiments are not properly scientific research.

Speaking as an active sound artist, one of the reasons for being interested in debunking the myths that are put about by EVP researchers is that, alongside the prevalence of EVP imagery in mainstream popular culture, throughout the period from the mid-1990s to the present day, EVP research has remained a theme within the repertoire of a significant number of electronic musicians and sound artists. A number of prominent artists have bluntly stated (sometimes verbally, sometimes also in print) that they literally believe in the supernatural provenance of EVP, while others have said that in effect they simply don't care whether the wild claims made by EVP researchers are factually true or not. So, while the desire to pro-actively debunk Spiritualist beliefs led the earlier *Rorschach Audio* publications and lectures etc to focus on the psychology of perception and philosophy-of-science aspects of this critique, there should be no doubt that the *Rorschach*

Audio project always was also a critique of the concepts, philosophies, beliefs and practices embodied in and expressed by certain forms of contemporary art.

The very earliest of this project's publications contained (quite influential) passages comparing EVP to the use of radio voices in the plot and sound effects of the Surrealist artist Jean Cocteau's cinematic masterpiece *Orphée*, and this project also drew attention to a frequently neglected passage from the notebooks of no less an artist than Leonardo Da Vinci, which discussed illusions of human voices emerging from the sound of pealing church bells, drawing an obvious comparison with the experiences alluded to in the vernacular poem *London Bells* ("Oranges and Lemons, say the bells of St Clements"). Similarly, one of the central texts quoted by this project has been a memo circulated within the BBC Monitoring Service during WW2, which discussed psychology of projection in relation to hearing. The memo in question was written by Monitoring Supervisor EH Gombrich, and *Rorschach Audio* is unique in emphasising the influence that wartime intelligence work with *sound* had on EH Gombrich's postwar masterpiece *Art and Illusion* – a book which is arguably one of the most important works of *visual* arts theory ever published.

In this context it probably comes as no surprise to say that a project which pointed out to artists themselves, to other arts professionals and to the general public, that most of the claims made by EVP researchers are factual nonsense, was inevitably going to ruffle a few feathers, not only among EVP enthusiasts, but also among those in the arts who have used EVP imagery to, bluntly but honestly, mostly pad-out the conceptual repertoire underpinning what is in many cases none too inspired sound art, rather than to say anything particularly profound or useful about the nature of human perception or about bereavement, for instance. When it comes to EVP, misleading the general public about this subject has proven quite popular, while, predictably, telling the truth has proven a good deal more controversial; and where *Rorschach Audio* explained why there was no (technical or spiritual) *Breakthrough* in the book of that name published by EVP researcher Konstantin Raudive (quite apart from the non-trivial issue of the resulting sound art inevitably being a bit dull) this critique also showed why there is no equivalent breakthrough in *artists* placing microphones in empty rooms to try to record voices of dead people either.

A common reaction from within the arts community to genuinely critical appraisals of EVP has been the counter-argument that EVP experimenters are or were, in effect, creative artists, producing, through their audio experimentation, forms of sound art and poetry. As EH Gombrich argued in *Art and Illusion*, the faculty for creating and appreciating art seems to be inherent to, and to therefore extend from, fundamental mechanisms of human perception, and therefore all people share creative faculties which are in that sense artistic (to a greater or lesser extent). However, while I totally agree with the common-sense idealism expressed in Gombrich's view of creativity, realistically speaking to say that in effect all people are artists does not necessarily mean that all people are either good or interesting artists, by any stretch of the imagination. In relation to poetry at least, as Jean-Paul Sartre wrote in his magnum-opus *Saint Genet*, "anyone can write bad verses" [1]; nonetheless, as a case in point, EVP researcher Raymond Cass was fond of implying (sometimes with a little encouragement from interviewers) that his relationship with the great poet Philip Larkin, might confer some sort of aesthetic credibility on his own EVP recordings. In fact the relationship was that Raymond Cass had worked as an audiologist who fitted hearing aids for Philip Larkin in Hull. Similarly, the 7-inch record published with Konstantin Raudive's book *Breakthrough* somewhat comically invoked the ghost of the Futurist poet Vladimir Mayakovsky; and, although not a poet, EVP researcher Friedrich Jürgenson was also, after all, a real artist – a figurative portrait painter who received a Papal Medal for the pictures he painted of several Popes.

So, a common response has been to side-step evidence that debunks EVP from the points-of-view of common-sense and of empirical knowledge, and to counter-claim that critics of EVP – like myself – are either insensitive to or in fact misunderstand the aesthetic qualities which embody the true value of EVP recordings. Berlin based critic Thibaut De Ruyter wrote for instance about what he termed "Aesthetic Voice Phenomena" for a special sound art supplement of the experimental music journal *Resonance*, stating that, in his assessments of EVP recording, his aim was "not to prove the veracity of these accounts or to accuse people who acted in good faith of hocus pocus", because "the idea here is to listen to these recordings…

in order to establish an aesthetic and a discourse regarding the intrinsic beauty of white noise" [2]. EVP recordings are not white noise as such (although they may contain white noise), and the core "idea" of EVP research does not seem to have had anywhere near as much to do with aesthetics as it has instead overwhelmingly focussed (time and time again, over a period of many decades) on trying to convince the public that dead people use domestic appliances to try to have conversations with us. Equally, for Thibaut De Ruyter to assume that all of the EVP researchers who tried to convince us of this did so in "good faith" is charitable of him to say the very least. De Ruyter goes on to assert that it is (apparently) "*bad* teachers" (emphasis added) who quote Leonardo Da Vinci's advice to novice painters, before volunteering the somewhat contradictory claim that "the poetry (and therefore the beauty) of EVP lies in its potentiality", because EVP "takes the listener into a world of possibilities, making him (sic) hear something that no doubt does not exist, but letting him believe that it is possible" – the obvious riposte would be to point out that the same argument could just as easily be used in defence of teaching Leonardo's advice.

Rather than relating to rational analyses of relevant evidence as empowering or as liberating experiences, De Ruyter offers the highly ideologically charged assertion that "EVP leaves whoever is listening *free* to recognise (and therefore to believe), rather than *battering* him with evidence" (emphases added), as if asking members of the public to consider relevant evidence was somehow tantamount to some form of *assault*; and this evidence is anyway, we are told, "desperately trivial". Given his misgivings about the advisability of questioning EVP research, it is all the more surprising that, in discussing an obvious comparison between EVP recording and its direct visual equivalent in (mostly Victorian) spirit photography, De Ruyter acknowledged "the obviousness of the fabrication, the feebleness of the photographic trickery" and "the cheap staging", and that he even goes so far as to openly admit that "it is hard not to laugh" at the "candour and naivety" of Spiritualist photographers. In stark contrast to his frank appraisal of the shortcomings of spirit photography, De Ruyter seems however to have been taken-in by EVP researchers' equally obvious trickery, because, in comparison to what he calls the "incense and thick curtains... the shadows... the sham costumes and the fairground ambience" of spirit photography, he seems to have fallen hook, line and sinker for what he calls "the clean and scientific" imagery of EVP. It is this "clean and scientific" imagery which De Ruyter believes shows EVP is a phenomenon "explored by serious people". Similarly, and echoing this train of thought, a manifesto published by a group called the International Necronautical Society was one of several art projects to echo the *Rorschach Audio* publications' observations about Jean Cocteau, with however the INS referring to listening by Raudive and Jürgenson as that conducted by "the scientist".

Curator and music journalist Daniela Cascella writes in the same issue of *Resonance* that the work of Swedish sound artist and EVP promoter CM von Hausswolff "challenges us with a paradox that baffles conventional modes of perception" [3], although, for the reasons described in detail in the earlier *Rorschach Audio* publications, it definitely does not. Similarly, both the method described in, and indeed the very title of Raudive's 1971 book *Breakthrough*, were both reproduced for an exhibit by the sound artist Scanner at Sheffield's Site Gallery in 2004, which announced its own *Breakthrough*, no less than 33 years after Raudive's original (self-titled) *Breakthrough*. Finally, in an interview entitled *A Fruitful Incoherence* the artist Susan Hiller relates feminist imperatives and post-colonial theory, albeit indirectly, to another artwork "based on Raudive's experiments when he left tape recorders running in empty, silent rooms and... then amplified the silence, discovering audible ghostly, voices" [4]. In the interview Susan Hiller states that Raudive's recordings provide "a very compelling metaphor for the kind of things that interest me, wanting to find the space between... the sound in the silence, the meaningful in nonsense", and she confirms that "I don't want either to debunk or to approve of his findings". While acknowledging that Susan Hiller's take on EVP is considerably more circumspect than some in contemporary art, nonetheless Hiller defines what she refers to as "the realm of the primitive" as encompassing the "home of supernatural beings... mysterious powers... lands of the dead, fabulous monsters", and she relates notions of "the other" (derived from post-colonial theory) and "arguments around the position of the feminine within art practice" to the "irrational, anarchic and untheorised", linking this train of thought to Raudive's EVP recordings. These connections are all made despite the self-evident masculinity of Raudive and most other leading EVP researchers, despite Raudive and Jürgenson's none too feminist nor post-colonial Roman Catholicism, and despite Raudive's relentless attempts to self-theorise his own work as though it was properly scientific research.

So, in summary, an obvious counter-argument to any "aesthetic" defence of EVP would be to point out that just as all people are easily capable of producing uninteresting art, similarly all belief systems, no matter how irrational (or, in some cases, even anti-social) they might be, can attract adherents because of at least some aesthetic aspect or quality (and I'll leave it to the imagination of this book's readers to visualise some other belief systems that draw-in followers because they too have strong *aesthetic* components). Of course it is the case however that *Rorschach Audio* publications have encouraged people to apply arguments from EH Gombrich's *Art and Illusion* to sound art, in much the same way that those arguments have, more conventionally, been applied to visual art; so, using the same arguments, it can indeed be said that false meanings projected onto ambiguous voices by EVP researchers definitely are artistic, because (on a perceptual level) these interpretations are also creative. Reiterating Sartre's statement about bad poetry however, the important point here is that EVP researchers are unfortunately no *more* creative than anyone else. The critical theorist Steven Connor asserts for instance that there are apparently bored shop staff who take pleasure in knowing customers tend to mishear the words "fuck you" as though what had actually been said to them was "thank you" [5], with (in this context) the obvious implication that it is those customers' expectations of being treated with polite respect that cause them to (creatively) mishear what they had every right to expect. Reductio-ad-absurdum, no-one would argue on that basis that either the staff or their victims are therefore artists, to any degree that would make that observation meaningful, so to an extent it's really a moot point to even discuss EVP research in such terms at all. The pertinent question is not whether or not EVP researchers can be considered to be artists, any more so than whether any of the rest of us are artists when for instance we apply creativity to choosing interior decorations, to selecting clothes, or to interpreting sounds; the pertinent question to ask in this context is whether, as artists, EVP researchers are actually any good?

As discussed, it was no less an artist than Leonardo Da Vinci who wrote of the influence that what can nowadays be referred to as perceptual creativity had on his method for composing paintings, and great artists who've been influenced by similar illusions and ambiguities of perception include, among many others, William Hogarth (and his *Satire on False Perspective*), Hans Holbein (*The Ambassadors*), Samuel van Hoogstraten (and his extraordinary three-dimensional perspective box, which can be seen in London's National Gallery), and artists as diverse as MC Escher and the film-maker David Cronenberg (*Videodrome*). As pointed out in earlier writing, emotional themes explored in illusory paintings by the Surrealist artist Salvador Dalí show strong similarities to equivalent themes in EVP research – notably Dalí's *Portrait of my Dead Brother*. Following on from Leonardo, the British painter Alexander Cozens helped to promote the technique of using "rude black sketches" in his *Essay to Facilitate the Inventing of Landskips, intended for Students in the Art* published in 1759, and in *A New Method of Assisting the Invention in Drawing Original Compositions in Landscape* published in 1786. This technique was adopted by the wonderful painter Joseph Wright (aka "Wright of Derby") for his *Blot Drawing in the Manner of Alexander Cozens* and *Landscape Study Development from a Blot*, and the art historians Judy Egerton and Kim Sloan identify several paintings which Wright composed (again openly citing the source of his inspiration) using the same method [6].

The art theorist František Šmejkal points out that one artist who, nearly a century afterwards "set out along the road later followed by Surrealism, was not a painter, but a poet" – Victor Hugo, whose drawings "contain in embryo the two main techniques of Surrealism: graphic automatism and dream inspiration". Indeed (like Wright) the Surrealists openly acknowledged inspirations and influences on their movement, and not only that, they also chose to acknowledge Victor Hugo's influence *in print* [7]. Victor Hugo's drawings were "executed with whatever lay to hand – pen, brush, a piece of matchstick... soot" and splashes of "Indian ink... black coffee", and (according to Léon Daudet) even Hugo's own blood [8], and these marks "assumed the form of fantastic landscapes, hallucinatory silhouettes of castles, ruins, lighthouses and towers, or weird night scenes with gallows and hanged figures". Šmejkal states that "Hugo's imagination played equally freely with the metamorphosis of objects, transforming a salt-cellar into a fountain set in a lake, a severed head into a moon, an eye into a planet, or expanding a mushroom to the monstrous dimensions of an antediluvean creature". It has also been stated that Victor Hugo drew "during Spiritualist séances, in order to access his unconscious mind", a concept which, it has been pointed out, was "only later popularized by Sigmund Freud" [9]. In light of material which will be discussed later on in this book, it is, incidentally, also interesting (if only coincidentally significant) that Victor Hugo also used his visual art to further distinguish himself as a campaigner against the death penalty.

Unsurprisingly, František Šmejkal references both the Rorschach ink-blot tests and Leonardo da Vinci's advice, but Šmejkal also links Victor Hugo's drawings to works by Gustave Moreau and Odilon Redon – the fantastic painter of monstrous eyes – and to the Surrealist Max Ernst. In a state of hypnagogic reverie Max Ernst made rubbings with black lead on paper, using the textures of mainly wood but also other surfaces, to reveal what he described as "rocks, the sea and the rain, earthquakes, the Sphinx in her stable, the little tables around the earth, the palette of Caesar, false positions, a shawl of frost flowers" and "human heads, animals, (and) a battle that ended with a kiss".

Speaking as someone whose early years were spent in a timber house, and given that the semi-circular artefacts in wood grain are commonly referred to as "eyes", it's hardly surprising that much of my childhood was spent surrounded by fantastical menageries of imaginary faces. So, if only for personal reasons, I cannot not add that it was within this environment that my father was planning to publish a book on the drawings of Victor Hugo. My father's effects contain a folder of proposals, correspondence, photographs and cuttings relating to the book he was planning with the Surrealist group member, actor and (as luck would have it) Barnsbury resident Jacques Brunius, who (among many other achievements) had been assistant director to Luis Buñuel on the film *L'Age d'Or*. Jacques Brunius died tragically young, and unfortunately very soon after the start of this project, en route to a lecturing engagement at the Exeter Festival of Modern Arts in April 1967; and, although my dad maintained a life-long enthusiasm for Hugo's work, (having overcome considerable odds to fight his way into a career in graphic design) the success of my dad's other projects meant the planned book was, as a result, never realised [10]. An excellent replacement is *Shadows of a Hand – The Drawings of Victor Hugo*, published in 1998 [11].

Insofar as my own work has used the methodology of Leonardo Da Vinci, Joseph Wright and Victor Hugo etc, my art project Disinformation exhibits a video called *Spellbound*. Rather than using splashes of ink or damp-stained walls as screens for projecting imaginary images however, instead *Spellbound* uses an aerial photograph of the immense (as described by *TIME Magazine*) "splashy star" of liquefied glass that melted onto the desert sand at the Trinity test-site at Alamogordo, New Mexico, in 1945, after the world's first atom bomb test [12]. Cross-fading between original photographs by US Army photographers JJ Mike Michnovicz and Bernard Waldman, the *Spellbound* exhibit encourages viewers to (so-to-speak) "share" an illusion I'd seen in Bernard Waldman's photo – the image of a human eye (by implication the eye of Manhattan Project director J Robert Oppenheimer), melted into the epicentre of the huge crater left by the thermonuclear blast; quoting Saint Jerome – "the face is the mirror of the mind, and eyes, without speaking, confess the secrets of the heart". The video's title was inspired by one of Salvador Dalí's paintings for the dream sequence in Alfred Hitchcock's movie *Spellbound*, in which, using very similar imagery, and in the same year as the Trinity test, Salvador Dalí depicted a huge eye hovering in mid-air over a vast expanse of flat desert [13].

Both in terms of evolutionary biology and of developmental psychology, it is hardly surprising that images projected onto abstract or random visual forms show a marked tendency to be perceived as (among other images) eyes and faces, since smiles, lip movements and eye contacts are among the first and most intimate communications established between babies and their parents. So, in that sense, artists unconsciously search for images of faces etc amid visual noise for the same reason that everyone else does, because that's what we're all programmed to do – eyes and faces are the first images a child learns to (and indeed must learn to) recognise.

Moving on from such discussions of visual art, to the

subject of equivalent uses of sound by artists specifically, the psychologist Diana Deutsch's *High-Low* recording from 1995 (which I've used in lectures to demonstrate how the mind projects meanings onto ambiguous speech fragments such as EVP recordings) is strikingly similar to the recently restored Overture which introduces the Lettrist artist and writer Isidore Isou's remarkable feature film *Venom and Eternity* from 1951. According to new credits added to the Kino International DVD of this film, the Kino DVD is equivalent to a kind of director's cut, which "restored more than 30 minutes of... deleted footage... including the five minute Lettrist Choir" [14]. Where Diana Deutsch's recording was composed from endlessly-repeated fragments of her own voice, *Venom and Eternity* starts with a barrage of rapidly repeating voice sounds, apparently sung by the Lettrist Choir, for a near full five minutes over a completely black screen, before the movie's original credits announce that "the film you are about to see differs radically – to put it mildly – from any film ever made any time, any place" (with the choir continuing, with variations, for another six minutes). Although there's no evidence whether Isou's Overture was intended to induce acoustic illusions or not, the similarity between his work and Diana Deutsch's recording is striking, and if *Venom and Eternity* has not so far been acknowledged as an extraordinary example of relatively early experimental sound art, then it certainly deserves to be.

In terms of how discreet sounds can be heard articulating apparently divergent meanings, in 1944 a

19-year-old Japanese poet called Kimitake Hiraoka took a neutral sounding pen-name that, without altering its phonetic pronunciation, can be re-written into alternate symbols, meaning "mysterious devil tale, devil bewitched by death", eventally telling friends on his 30th birthday that "this is the real way" to write the name Yukio Mishima [15]. Yukio Mishima is widely recognised as one of Japan's most accomplished postwar authors, indeed he was nominated for the Nobel Prize three times, and it is tempting to speculate whether Mishima might have been influenced in his manner of choosing a pen-name by the extraordinary Japanese mystery, horror and detective fiction writer Hirai Tarō, who (decades previously) took the name Edogawa Rampo, on account of that name's phonetic similarity to the name of his idol Edgar Allan Poe [16] (incidentally one of Edogawa Rampo's stories is called *Shinri Shiken – The Psychological Test*, and, in Rampo's old age, certainly Mishima and Rampo personally met). Similarly, in 1985 the French burglar, prostitute, poet, novelist, playwright and activist Jean Genet mis-heard the sound "L'Amour" (love) as "La Mort" (death), in an interview conducted for BBC TV by the novelist and playwright Nigel Williams, shortly before Genet's own death [17].

As regards Jean Genet and Yukio Mishima, and as phenomena consistent with the concept of "Rorschach Audio" (namely with the idea that mishearings may reveal something of the mind-set or emotional disposition, reflected in their authors' conscious or subconscious mind) it would be hard to underestimate the importance of such imagery in the creative repertoire of artists who were certainly among the greatest writers of 20th century France and Japan. As an articulation of Jean-Paul Sartre's discourse on Genet's embodiment of "the negative", Sartre describes Genet's fixation with associations between love and death, quoting Genet as saying, years before the BBC interview, that "there must have been certain forces in my unconscious (complexes, childhood memories, desires, etc) which produced this association so regularly... it is because death must live within me... it springs forth from my slightest word" [18]. Recent artworks published by Disinformation draw comparisons between the homophonic ambiguities that preoccupied Genet and Mishima, and the visual illusion discovered by the 19th century Swiss crystallographer Louis Albert Necker [19].

Incidentally, both Jean Genet and Yukio Mishima were also highly accomplished short film-makers, and both were political activists. Genet supported (for instance) American Black Panthers and Palestinian activists, and Mishima proved to have been (to use his own words) so "bewitched" by death that he formed a tiny ultra-nationalist right-wing army, then committed suicide in 1970, after a symbolic but spectacularly unsuccessful attempt to overthrow Japanese democracy. Mishima's turn away from cosmopolitan values to the culture and politics of xenophobic militarism almost certainly had more to do with conflicts arising from his own sexuality than it had to do with Japanese politics or cultural identity; and, should anyone be tempted to romanticise his actions, it's worth remembering what Mishima's political legacy really is. When, for instance, British National Party representative Adam Walker visited Tokyo's notorious Yasukuni shrine, where over 1,000 convicted war criminals are venerated as divinities, the BNP visit was hosted by Nippon Issuikai – a small but influential hard-right group founded by veterans of Mishima's original private army. Despite working in Japan as an immigrant himself, Adam Walker is a former school teacher who resigned his job in 2007 after describing immigrants to the UK as "savage animals" and as "filth" [20][21]. Yukio Mishima was also closely involved with Japanese war crimes denier and racist Shintarō Ishihara, who, in case anyone thinks such politics are confined to the fringes of modern Japanese life, has been governor of Tokyo since 1999 [22].

Somewhat less politically controversial was the life of the writer, poet, and BBC Monitoring Service veteran Geoffrey Grigson, who, echoing the description of names heard emerging from sounds of church bells by Leonardo da Vinci, noted illusions of words emerging from bell-ringing, from bird calls and even from rotating mill wheels. Having a habit of befriending old timers in the village where he grew up in Cornwall, Geoffrey recalled that "one of the last millers in the neighbourhood of Pelynt first told me the proverb that *hair grows on the palm of the honest miller*, and the millstone he said clacked *for profit, for profit, for profit* when it was revolving fast, changing sadly and slowly to *no profit, no profit, no profit* when the water was turned off and the pace declined" [23]. Shadows of politics are never far behind however, as, irrespective of whether the following was ever meant to be taken literally, a miller I spoke to said that part of the mechanism was traditionally referred as "the damsel" because it talked so much. Geoffrey Grigson also compiled a poetry anthology which recounts such illusions in the world famous English poem *London Bells* [24], and EH Gombrich discussed similar illusions in his memo to the BBC Monitoring Service, describing the "mechanism by which we read familiar shapes into clouds, or melodies into the monotonous rattle of a train" [25].

Echoing aspects of this description by EH Gombrich, James Joyce's epic, dream-like and highly impressionistic experimental novel *Finnegans Wake*, which is absolutely crammed with acoustic word-play, tells of how "the night express sings his story" [26], and mis-heard train sounds provide central imagery in the Nilgiri writer and activist Indu K Mallah's beautiful book *Shadows in Dream Time*. *Shadows in Dream Time* describes a scene in which, during a long journey "the motion of the train had a soporific effect, and the sound of the wheels seemed to chant *flames and ashes, flames and ashes, flames and ashes*, and later on *broken wings, broken wings, broken wings*." This perception caused the narrator's mind to go back "to a game they had played as schoolgirls" in which "they would stand one behind the other, in a line, hands mimicking the motions of the train wheels, and would chant, first slowly, and then with increasing momentum *coffee, coffee, coffee... cheese n' biscuits, cheese n' biscuits, cheese n' biscuits... fish n' chips, fish n' chips, fish n' chips*, before finally imitating the whistle of the train". Indu Mallah states that it was "amazing how close it came to imitating the sound of a train when done well" [27].

Such illusions are subject to charming parody in the sound design for Walt Disney's sometimes wildly Surrealistic and hallucinatory film *Dumbo* – for whose production an innovative sound effects machine called the Sonovox was used to transform the whistling of a cute anthropomorphic steam train called Casey Junior into cries of "*All Abooooaaarrd*". The effort of Casey Junior chuffing up-hill transforms into a chant of (slowly) "*I think I can, I think I can, I think I can*", as the train struggles to reach the summit, after which Casey's free-wheeling down-hill sprint transforms into (quickly) "*I thought I could, I thought I could, I thought I could*" [28]. Wonderfully escapist as the artistry of *Dumbo* is, the art-of-life lies close at hand, as the real-life Casey Senior – the American railroad engineer Casey Jones – was pilloried as a strike breaker by IWW activist Joe Hill [29]. If any reader thinks discussing *Dumbo* strays too far from this chapter's brief for exploring links between "Rorschach Audio" type phenomena and art and literature, of course I believe that films like *Dumbo* are *proper* art, but either way the logic of this anecdote comes full circle anyway, as, recognising an obvious streak of mutual Surrealism, Salvador Dalí sought out Walt Disney in America, and spent several years working for Disney on an (until recently unfinished) co-production called *Destino* [30].

As for the actual mechanism of Sonovox effects, in his magnificent MIT Press published magnum-opus on *Auditory Scene Analysis*, the psychoacoustician Albert Bregman recalls that "as a boy, I used to hear a radio commercial put out by the Bromo-Seltzer company" which "consisted of a commercial message spoken by a steam powered train. First the whistle called out a slogan and then the name of the product was repeated over and over by the sound of the steam engine as it picked up speed. The sound of the engine was perfectly represented and so were the words". Albert Bregman rightly assumed that the illusion of the speaking train was created by "recording the train sounds, and then piping them into the vocal tract of a person while the words were being mouthed" [31] – in other words that this effect was almost certainly another product of the Sonovox.

In fact Casey Junior made an appearance in one other Disney production, in 1941 [32]. In a fascinating fictitious "real-life" documentary-within-a-cartoon called *The Reluctant Dragon*, a visitor is led on a tour of departments within Disney Studios, witnessing a musically-scored sound performance with Sonovox, bell, steam jets, cello, lawn-mower blades, piano, ukulele, bull horns, tuned glass jugs, snare drum, organ pipes, bubbles, balloons, metal sheet, cymbals, rain machine, balsa wood, razor, glass, mechanical noise machines and collapsing piles of steel buckets, which are used to create the soundtrack for a train crash experienced by Casey Junior. These effects make the fabulous Intonarumori of Futurist sound artist Luigi Russolo look frankly tame by comparison, and, as the visitor says, "wouldn't it be easier just to wreck a real train?" In *The Reluctant Dragon* the Sonovox is depicted as piping sounds from gramophone discs into small transducers which the operator holds against their vocal chords, to allow those sounds to be articulated using vocal intonations (the depiction in this sequence is almost certainly simplified, as the Sonovox must have been a little more complex than just that).

The genesis of this invention had in fact been described in 1939 by *TIME Magazine*, which reported how novelist Gilbert Wright (the son of the legendary American writer Harold Bell Wright) "made real people talk like waterfalls, braying donkeys, barking dogs, slamming doors, locomotive whistles" [33]. "Six months ago, while Gilbert Hunger Wright was meditatively scratching the bristly whiskers on his Adam's apple, he noticed that queer sounds came out of his mouth. When he silently mouthed words, the sounds caused by scratching his whiskers were formed into words. Fascinated, Gilbert Wright, who was once an engineer and radio operator, began to experiment further. Finally he came up with a device which his father... christened Sonovox. In the Sonovox, a sound recording of a waterfall, a vociferating animal, rattling dice or whatnot is fed through wires to two little biscuit-shaped gadgets which are placed on each side of the throat against the larynx. These gadgets transmit the sound vibrations to the larynx, so that the sound comes out of the throat as if produced there. The sound is shaped into speech by mouthing the desired words... Walt Disney, as might have been expected, immediately offered to buy the exclusive rights". Similar effects were later produced by devices such as the Talk Box and the Vocoder – the latter being a military speech encryption technology that was subsequently adapted for use by electronic musicians.

If, however, this discussion of Sonovox effects might

again seem to have strayed too far from that of genuine *Rorschach Audio* phenomena, because the Sonovox blends other sounds with actual (rather than imaginary) human voices, and was used (among other applications) to *suggest* to listeners that train sounds may sometimes resemble speech, rather than to *cause* listeners to mishear train sounds as speech, then it is worth pointing out that this sub-plot also returns our narrative to Spiritualism and to Electronic Voice Phenomena. As a case in point, a comedy horror film called *You'll Find Out* ("music gets mixed-up with murder") was made one year before *Dumbo*, in which the actor Bela Lugosi used vocal distortions produced by the Sonovox to create the voice of a ghost during a séance [34].

Obviously Lugosi's trick was designed purely for entertainment, but at least one similar device seems to have been used in contexts in which it was intended, however implausibly, to be taken seriously. As detailed in an excellent Channel 4 TV documentary directed by David Monaghan, an American "millionaire and industrialist" called George Meek "was inspired by Raudive's voices" and formed an organisation called Metascience Foundation. George Meek announced (on a promotional videotape) that "I am a visionary, and here is my vision". Metascience promoted a newly invented EVP machine called Spiricom, built by "electronic technician and psychic" William O'Neill, allegedly in consultation with the ghost of a scientist called Dr George Mueller. The Spiricom device was described as enabling direct real-time exchanges of conversation between the living and the dead. During Easter 1982 Meek held a PR event at The National Press Club in Washington DC, announcing to the assembled media that "for many Christians our findings may be one of the most significant items of news in 2,000 years", and describing the Metascience findings as "truly fantastic and far-out". Although many EVP researchers had made these exact claims before, George Meek went on to announce that "for the first time we have *electronic proof* that the mind, memory banks and personality survive death" (emphases added), and, despite being heckled for asking the media to believe such a "cock and bull story", the conference is said to have "made international headlines". As described by Spiricom researcher Sarah Estep "George took the Spiricom system and went to many countries around the world", and "when people would hear these sample tapes... they would buy the Spiricom manual... (and) they would build it". As Sarah Estep repeatedly stressed however "no-one, no-one in the world, *no-one* had the results with Spiricom as William O'Neill is given credit for having" (emphasis not added). As EVP researcher Alexander McCrae observed, the kind of sounds recorded on the Metascience demonstration cassettes "can be very easily faked", and Spiricom was widely ridiculed, even among EVP enthusiasts, after it became apparent that the tapes' characteristic vocal sound was remarkably similar to a vintage children's LP called *Sparky's Magic Piano*, which had been recorded in 1948 using the Sonovox [35].

So, while examples such as Jean Genet, Geoffrey Grigson, Isidore Isou, Yukio Mishima, Edogawa Rampo and Gilbert Wright (and no doubt many others) provide plenty of anecdotal evidence of literary figures taking an interest in aspects of mishearing and ambiguous speech perception, and while Indu Mallah (and almost certainly James Joyce) used related phenomena to provide important literary imagery, as for exploiting such phenomena as a *systematic* strategy for developing literary creativity, the Surrealist film-maker Georges Hugnet described "a universe of strange mechanisms, mysterious accessories, prodigious inventions (and) enormous vertigo" in the "strange and unique case" of an author who "in his solitude has slowly and imperturbably built up his kingdom like an antheap", leaving what can realistically be said, even today, to be "a human document of the highest importance". Georges Hugnet wrote that "the sun of Raymond Roussel is unforgiving", and stated that whoever enters Raymond Roussel's world "returns Spellbound" [36]. It's not made totally clear in an article in *Variant* magazine whether it was Michel Foucault or Alain Robbe-Grillet who said that Raymond Roussel was an author whose "life and work are *so unusual* that for a long time some people believed him to be a fictional character" (emphasis added). Indeed, Raymond Roussel (1877-1933) was a man so strange, that, according to legend, and among many eccentricities, he travelled the world without ever leaving the comfort of his luxury mobile home (the "automobile roulotte", from which, as a result, he is sometimes credited as having invented the Winnebago) [37].

Raymond Roussel was a French aristocrat whose

enormous inheritance enabled him to self-publish extraordinary novels and to stage their theatrical dramatisations. Roussel's work was pilloried by critics, mocked by audiences, and rejected by virtually all of his literary and theatrical contemporaries, with the notable exception of those early Surrealists who, while exploiting Roussel's generosity to help deplete their friend's financial resources, in the cases of André Breton and Louis Aragon at least, nonetheless lionised Roussel as a major influence on the development of Surrealist art. Indeed, 28 years after the publication of Roussel's novel *Impressions of Africa*, a painting that takes that novel's name was created by Salvador Dalí [38].

The relevance of Raymond Roussel's work to the concept of *Rorschach Audio* lies in the fact that much of his literary oeuvre was created by extrapolating narratives from images suggested by wordplay based on mishearings. A common theme in contemporary sound art is the practice of creating "generative" (self-composing) electronic music, and, by comparison, Roussel's work was effectively a form of generative (although still highly personal, in that sense non-mechanised) literature. Georges Hugnet recalls that "to find the subject of an anecdote, Roussel used to choose a phrase, any phrase, ready made". Then Roussel would "repeat it to himself until other words, by similarity of sound, appeared under the others", creating similar perceptions to those experienced when listening to Diana Deutsch's *High-Low* recording. Roussel then "noted the words so found, sought a connection between them, and from this took his story". So the words "Napoléon premier empereur" (the first Emperor Napoleon) metamorphosed into "Nappe ollé miettes hampe air heure" (slick Olé crumbs shaft air time), which became (no kidding) "the basis of a story", showing how Roussel "induced inspiration" and revealing "the whole paranoiac system in which he lived". Roussel's methodology is exemplified by the title of his novel *Impressions of Africa* – a self-mocking joke derived from mishearing the term "Impression A Fric", which (we are told) is traditionally printed on the frontispiece of French books to indicate when they have been "published at the author's own expense", as indeed were all of Roussel's publications.

As for the psychoanalytical metaphor implicit in the concept of "Rorschach Audio", owing to obvious issues relating to French to English translation, and to the oblique nature of much of Raymond Roussel's imagery, on the surface it's hard to be certain whether Roussel's work contains much content than can be definitely attributed to conscious or unconscious self-expressions, revealed through the nature of their author's mishearings and auditory projections. However it is tempting to speculate that Roussel's fictitious Professor Martial Canterel may to some extent be a projection of autobiographical fantasy, not to mention a projection of wishful-thinking. Roussel imagines Professor Canterel as the owner of a fantastic estate called Locus Solus, which gives its name to one of Roussel's novels. The novel describes a place where, "surrounded by disciples full of passionate admiration for his continual discoveries, who lend their enthusiastic support", Professor Canterel "devotes his entire life to science", working in "luxurious model laboratories". Raymond Roussel describes Professor Canterel as a "bachelor with no commitments whose large fortune at once removes any material difficulties incurred by the various targets he sets himself", and as a man of "marvellous intellect", with a "warm, pervasive voice (which) lent great charm to his engaging delivery, whose seductiveness and precision made him a master of the spoken word" [39]. Roussel was indeed a bachelor with no commitments and a large fortune, who craved the admiration and support of sometimes fickle disciples. However, as to the products of Roussel's intellect, such self-flattery could be pompous and boring, were it not for the fact that the discoveries produced by Roussel's linguistic "science" were every bit as marvellous, warm, seductive and precise as any prose could probably hope to be under such circumstances.

As an illustration of Raymond Roussel's prodigious gift for seductive and beguiling imagery, Roussel describes Professor Canterel as having discovered an extraordinary liquid called Aqua Micans, which "thanks to a special, very potent oxygenation... enabled any terrestrial creature whatsoever, human or animal, to live fully submerged without interrupting its respiration", and Roussel could almost be describing his own prose when he describes "the most striking peculiarity of this water" as being "its astounding brilliance". Indeed, in one respect at least, Roussel's fantasy anticipated real experiments conducted by the American biochemist Leland Clark more than half a century later [40], and Aqua Micans bears a startling resemblance to the perfluorocarbon oxygen-carrier

Oxycyte that Professor Clark invented – in the real world [41]. As for Aqua Micans, "the smallest drop shone with blinding light and seemed, even in the shade, to sparkle with a fire of its own", and Roussel goes on to detail a scenario so extraordinary it is amazing that more seems not to have been made of this imagery in terms of concepts for cinema and audio installation art. A dancer "celebrated for the beautiful harmony of her poses" breathes, submerged inside the "photogenic tide" of a giant glass diamond filled with Aqua Micans and illuminated by bright sunlight. Then "because of the excessive amounts of oxygen she was absorbing... her hair began to give out a vague resonance which swelled or died away according to the amplitude of her head movements", producing "strange music" from "hair vibrating like the strings of an instrument... with a compass extending over more than three octaves" – hair that was "strongly electrified" and which combined "great acoustical power with incomparable luminosity".

As (the real) Leland Clark experimented with anaesthetised mice, (the fictitious) Professor Canterel then decides to experiment with a "white Siamese tom-cat named Khóng-dek-lèn". An old-fashioned kitchen-sink science demonstration involves bending a thin stream of smoothly-flowing tap water in mid-air, with a biro that's been charged with static electricity by rubbing it in hair (it really works), so it's plausible that Roussel, like the inventor Nikola Tesla and the artist Louis Wain, may also have been fascinated by electrification and by the minute static sparking that can sometimes be seen in cat fur in the dark. In comparison to the much longer hair of the dancer, and as a musical bio-instrument, the electrical activity of the cat's much shorter hair produced only "a feeble and confused hum". Then, however, the cat's fur began to visibly phosphoresce, leaving the animal "surrounded by dazzling, lambent flames", and giving the Professor electric shocks when he reached in to remove Khóng-dek-lèn from the liquid inside the giant glass diamond [42].

Alongside these extraordinary musical inventions, Raymond Roussel then imagines the creation of an equally fantastical fictitious phonograph, whose purpose was in essence to create sounds very similar to EVP. In *Locus Solus* Roussel describes another character called Lucius Egroizard, who, equally serendipitously, he also imagines to have been an "enthusiastic member of Italian society exclusively devoted to the cult of Leonardo Da Vinci". Lucius Egroizard became insane after seeing his daughter Gillette murdered by a band of Kentish bandits called the Red Gang, and, "believing himself to be Leonardo Da Vinci, the wretched man connected his universal speculations in art and science with his daughter, the thought of whom obsessed him". Taking pity on the poor man, Professor Canterel rescued Egroizard from an insane asylum, and, to relieve the bereaved father's madness, the Professor provided Egroizard with a laboratory and research materials, with which to create a "remarkable invention" for the "artificial creation of speech or song", in order to "reproduce his daughter's voice as it had been manifested to his attentive ear... during the last days of her life". So, imagining a research project that quite closely anticipates real psychoacoustics, Speech Synthesis and EVP experiments, "using an infinite variety of timbres and intonations, he created all kinds of components from fragments of conversations or tunes, hoping that, among so many elements, he might chance upon some sonorous indication capable of setting him on the right path". With his new phonograph eventually completed, Egroizard finally "slid the point of the reproducing needle over the new line" ("line" presumably meaning the groove in the gramophone disc) "and from the very bottom of the horn, on the vowel "A", emerged a long, merry syllable", which is described as "recalling the smiling first efforts of very young children eager to talk". Lucius Egroizard cries out "it's her voice... my daughter's voice!... it's you, my Gillette... they haven't killed you... you're here... beside me"; and "between these disjointed sentences came, like a response, the first attempt at a word, which he constantly reproduced". The thematic similarity between the tragic scenario imagined by Raymond Roussel and post-war EVP researchers' investigations into electronic Spiritualism could hardly in fact be much closer [43].

So, to conclude this chapter, in terms of the genuinely great art that has been created by those artists who were fascinated by and who explored and exploited the subtlety and creative potential of ambiguities of speech perception and of hearing, it seems highly appropriate that both the compositional methodology and the content of Raymond Roussel's extraordinary prose so closely reflect the themes and methods that would subsequently be misunderstood by postwar EVP researchers; and, finally, and with apologies for ending on such a grim note, ground down by decades of rejection by the public and by most critics and artists, Raymond Roussel committed suicide on 14 July 1933, bankrupt, dejected, and surrounded by empty barbiturate bottles [44].

[1] Jean-Paul Sartre *Saint Genet – Actor and Martyr*, WH Allen, London, 1964, p.429
[2] Thibaut De Ruyter "Aesthetic Voice Phenomena" in Anna Colin (editor) *Sound Art*, London Musicians Collective, 2005, pp.37-42
[3] Daniela Cascella "Blind Sound" in Anna Colin, op.cit., p.63
[4] Susan Hiller & Gavin Jantjes *A Fruitful Incoherence: Dialogues with Artists on Internationalism* Institute of International Visual Arts, London, 1998, pp.20-31
[5] Steven Connor "Earslips: Of Mishearings and Mondegreens" in "Listening In, Feeding Back" conference, Columbia University, Feb 2009, transcript p.10
[6] Judy Egerton *Wright of Derby* Tate Gallery, London, 1990, pp.138-139 & p.142
[7] František Šmejkal *Surrealist Drawings* Artia, Prague, 1974, and Octopus, London, 1975, pp.14-15 & p.20
[8] Léon Daudet "Le Voyage de Shakespeare" 1896, quoted in Pierre Georgel "The Artist in Spite of Himself" in Florian Rodari, Pierre Georgel, Luc Sante and Marie-Laure Prévost *Shadows of a Hand – The Drawings of Victor Hugo*, Merrell, London, 1998, p.18
[9] http://en.wikipedia.org/wiki/Victor_Hugo – accessed 7/12/11

[10] Colin Banks, Jacques Brunius, John Miles & others, correspondence February 1967 to April 1968
[11] Léon Daudet "Le Voyage de Shakespeare" 1896, quoted in Pierre Georgel *The Artist in Spite of Himself* in Florian Rodari et.al., op.cit., p.18
[12] *TIME Magazine*, 17 September 1945, p.68
[13] Robert Descharnes & Gilles Néret *Dalí* Taschen, Cologne, 1997, p.391
[14] Jean Isidore Isou *Venom and Eternity* (*Traité de Bave et D'Eternité*) 1951, on *Avant-Garde 2: Experimental Films 1928-1954* Kino International DVD, July 2007
[15] John Nathan *Mishima – A Biography* Hamish Hamilton, London, 1975, p.122
[16] http://en.wikipedia.org/wiki/Edogawa_Rampo – accessed 10/2/12
[17] Jean Genet, interviewed by Nigel Williams *Arena* BBC TV, 12 Nov 1985
[18] Jean-Paul Sartre *Saint Genet – Actor and Martyr* WH Allen, London, 1964, p.438
[19] Disinformation *Portrait of Jean Genet* 2011 – www.flickr.com/photos/disinfo/6152976826/ and video installation
[20] Leigh Phillips & Justin McCurry "BNP Attends International Far Right Conference in Japan" *The Guardian*, 11 August 2010
[21] Graeme Paton "BNP Teacher Described Immigrants as Filth" *Daily Telegraph*, 24 May 2010
[22] http://en.wikipedia.org/wiki/Shintaro_Ishihara – accessed 1/2/11

[23] Geoffrey Grigson *Freedom of the Parish* Phoenix House, London, 1954

[24] Geoffrey Grigson (editor) *The Cherry Orchard* Phoenix House, London, 1959

[25] EH Gombrich "Some Axioms, Musings and Hints on Hearing" quoted in Joe Banks "Rorschach Audio" in *Leonardo Music Journal* vol.11, The MIT Press, 2001, pp.77-83

[26] James Joyce *Finnegans Wake* Faber & Faber, London, 1939, 1, 1.6, 135

[27] Indu K Mallah *Shadows in Dream Time* Affiliated East-West Press, Madras, 1990, pp.47-48 & 110

[28] Ben Sharpsteen *Dumbo* Walt Disney Studios, 1941

[29] http://en.wikipedia.org/wiki/Joe_Hill – accessed 7/12/11

[30] Robert Descharnes & Gilles Néret, op.cit., p.393

[31] Albert Bregman *Auditory Scene Analysis* MIT Press, 1990, p.610

[32] Alfred Werker *The Reluctant Dragon* Walt Disney Studios, 1941

[33] *TIME Magazine*, Monday 24 July 1939

[34] http://en.wikipedia.org/wiki/Sonovox – accessed 7/12/11

[35] Assorted videotapes and interviews etc in David Monaghan *Witness – Voices of the Dead* Channel 4, 2001

[36] Georges Hugnet "1870 to 1936" in Herbert Read (editor) *Surrealism* Faber & Faber, london 1936, pp.243-244

[37] C O'Farrell "Foucault: Historian or Philosopher?" Macmillan, London, 1989, quoted in William Clark "A Lovely Curiosity – Raymond Roussel" *Variant* 15, 2002, pp.5-9

[38] Robert Descharnes & Gilles Néret, op.cit., pp.302-303
[39] Raymond Roussel *Locus Solus* translated by Rupert Copeland Cuningham, John Calder, London, 1983, p.5
[40] Allen Bollands "An Artificial Alternative to Blood" *New Scientist*, 17 September 1987, p.67
[41] http://www.oxycyte.com – retrieved 30 January 2012
[42] Raymond Roussel, op.cit., pp.63-66
[43] Raymond Roussel, op.cit., pp.195-204
[44] William Clark, op.cit., pp.5-9

ACKNOWLEDGEMENTS

This chapter is based on an article called "Rorschach Audio – All Aboard!" which appears in *The Book of Guilty Pleasures*, edited by Song-Ming Ang and Kim Cascone, Circadian Songs, 2011, and on a lecture presented to The Institute for Modern and Contemporary Culture, The University of Westminster, London, 7 December 2011. Special thanks to Song-Ming Ang and Kim Cascone, to David Cunningham and Chris Daley for arranging the lecture, and to Caroline and Colin Banks, Poulomi Desai, Geoffrey Grigson, and to Chris and Tatiana Patten for various gifts and loans of research materials.

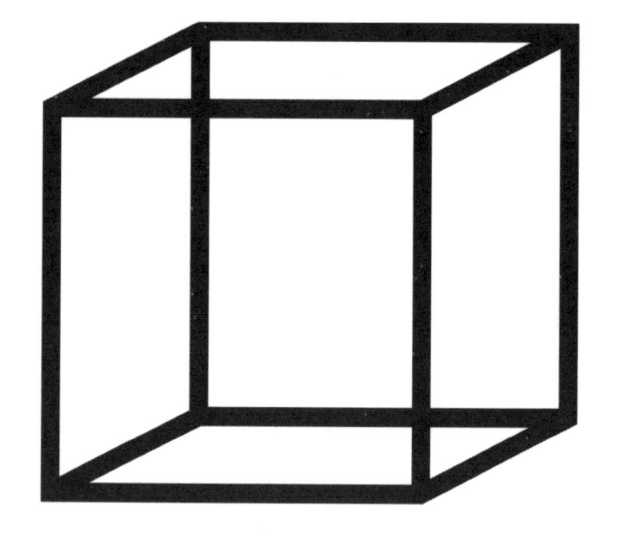

"Let Him Have It, Chris!"

Artwork by Disinformation © September 2011

Chapter 4
Let Him Have It, Chris!

"The central nervous system is nature's Sistine Chapel, but we have to bear in mind that the world our senses present to us – this office, my lab, our awareness of time – is a ramshackle construct which our brains have devised to let us get on with the job of maintaining ourselves and reproducing our species. What we see is a highly conventionalised picture, a simple tourist guide to a very strange city. We need to dismantle this ramshackle construct in order to grasp what's really going on."
– JG Ballard, 1992 [1]

"You people with eyes, you're so busy looking you never notice anything" – Philip MacDonald, 1956 [2]

Issues surrounding the subject of mishearing may, at first glance, seem relatively incidental to discourse relating to major cultural issues in contemporary society and visual culture. After all, well-known so-called Mondegreens, whereby unclear lyrics sung by pop musicians and other recording artists are misinterpreted as a variety of often comical homophones, are hardly the stuff of major public controversy (one personal favourite comes from a friend who misheard the lyrics to the song *Alternative Ulster* by the Irish punk band Stiff Little Fingers, as "A Man and a Lobster") [3]. Indeed, my own reflexive recourse to the use of terms like "first glance" shows (at least anecdotally) how language itself can reflect tendencies to form concepts around visual images. In fact, in context of this discussion, one irony of using a form like written language, based as it is on, to paraphrase Aristotle's *Poetics*, symbolic visual representations of indivisible sounds [4], is that it is virtually impossible to even discuss the subject of mishearing without invoking concepts, symbols and metaphors which are themselves derived from visual culture. As above, one constructs a sentence highlighting the irony of how a statement about hearing makes use of visual imagery, and that sentence itself makes use of even more visual imagery (the further examples in this case being the use of the words "shows" and "reflect", in addition to the previous use of the term "first glance"); and the rest of this article will no doubt be filled with further examples of that paradox.

The tendency of the human perceptual system (like, arguably, culture itself) to prefer, to prioritise and to value visual information over many of its auditory counterparts, is further demonstrated by a classic perceptual psychology experiment known as The McGurk Effect, in which test volunteers were asked watch a videotape of the face of a speaker who has been filmed repeating monosyllabic sounds. The original speaker was filmed repeating the syllable "ga", however what viewers are presented with is a version of that video which has been dubbed, so that the syllable "ga" has been removed from the video soundtrack and replaced with the syllable "ba" (and this replacement sound is synchronised with the lip movements of the original speaker). What test subjects then hear as a result is in fact neither "ga" nor "ba", but instead they hear the syllable "da", which is phonetically in between "ba" and "ga" [5][6]. The McGurk Effect demonstration is readily accessible on YouTube [7], and becomes most impressive when viewers realise that the sound they hear actually changes depending on whether or not their eyes are open or closed. When their eyes are closed, listeners accurately perceive the dubbed soundtrack "ga", but when their eyes open, and their perceptions are influenced by deliberately misleading visual disinformation, the mind resolves the discrepancy between the contradictory sound and vision by hearing the sound "da" as a subjectively "real" interpretation of the actual sound carried from the video monitor across the room to their ears. In other words, the visual information partially over-rides, takes precedence over, and modifies the auditory information, in the formation of the perceived sound that the mind then (so-to-speak) "projects" into the environment as being "real".

The McGurk Effect suggests not only that there is an underlying physiological basis for some forms of such visual precedence, but it also suggests that lip-reading is an integral component in normal speech perception as well (as much as lip-reading is more obviously of use to deaf people and to the hard of hearing). Indeed, *New Scientist* magazine quoted a correspondent who reported that, similarly, "he heard better when wearing his spectacles", and who concluded that "seeing the mouth movements of the speaker can be as useful an aid to hearing as sound amplification" [8]. Indeed, the fact that most listeners rely in their hearing to a greater or lesser extent on some degree of ability to read lips and faces is also demonstrated by vernacular popular culture. It is apparently (although for no obvious reason) most common in Scotland that people tease each other by mouthing the phrases "Elephant Shoe" and "Olive Juice" across perceptually, if not "silent", then certainly "foggy" spaces, such as typically noisy pubs and bars, with their lip movements being mis-read as the words "I Love You", as evidently the lip movements for these different phrases are all virtually identical; and in fact this phenomenon is even immortalised as the title of an album by the Scottish rock group Arab Strap [9]. Similarly, as long ago as 1912 the Principal of the New York School for the Hard of Hearing, Edward Nitchie, wrote that, after sufficient instruction in the art of lip-reading, "with the eye thus trained it often happens that the lip-readers' impression is that of actually hearing what is said", and Nitchie encouraged his students to "use ears and eyes in fullest co-operation", reporting that as a result of learning to lip-read "pupils have reported... an actual betterment of hearing" [10]. The ability of visual information to improve the accuracy of hearing was also described by none other than the physicist who "invented" the electrical quantity we refer to as Amps – André-Marie Ampere, who observed that, when listening to opera "if the words are not pronounced loudly, the listener seated at the back of the hall receives only the impression of the vowels and musical modulations, but... does not recognise the words. Let him then open the libretto and follow [the printed lyrics] along with his eyes; he will hear very distinctly the same articulations that a little while ago he was unable to grasp" [11]. As described in earlier *Rorschach Audio* articles, the South African poet David Wright's ability to lip-read is reported to be so powerful that he described continuing to perceive lip movements as producing (subjectively speaking) real sounds, even after he became profoundly deaf [12].

If examples such as these may shed some light on why it is that the phenomenology of visual culture is sometimes perceived as being more important than its auditory equivalents, with regard to even more obviously cultural issues however, few incidents could illustrate the importance of mishearing as a focus of contention in genuinely world-changing cultural and political debates than events which surrounded a warehouse robbery that took place in Croydon, South London, in November 1952. Without going into excessive detail, two young criminals, Christopher Craig and (former bin-man and street cleaner) Derek Bentley, were in the process of burgling a confectionary warehouse on the Tamworth Road, when they were interrupted by the arrival of the Croydon police. Detective Sergeant Fred Fairfax detained Bentley, who, it is alleged, wrestled free and called out the now infamous words "Let him have it, Chris". Rather than handing over his gun to the police officer, Chris Craig shot Sergeant Fairfax with a sawn-off pistol, but Fairfax survived and then arrested Derek Bentley. Chris Craig fired a second shot, tragically killing Police Constable Sidney Miles. As the shooter Chris Craig was, at the time of the offence, aged 16, therefore below the age of criminal responsibility, and despite substantial opposition from Members of Parliament and protests by members of the public, it was the 19-year-old Derek Bentley who was executed for murder just two months later in January 1953, despite the fact that Bentley had not fired the gun, and although he had in fact been under arrest when the fatal shot had been fired. The case is described in detail in David Yallop's book *To Encourage the Others* [13], is the subject of numerous protest songs, and is dramatised in the film *Let Him Have It* directed by Peter Medak [14].

Public concern about the execution of a young man who was epileptic, of unusually low intelligence, and who had not fired the fatal shot, was fed by inconsistencies in the ballistics evidence, by uncertainty as to whether Derek Bentley even knew whether Chris Craig was carrying a gun, and by uncertainties concerning the interpretation of the phrase "Let him have it". Although Craig and Bentley both denied these words had ever been spoken, the prosecution considered this phrase to have been an instruction from Bentley to Craig to shoot Fairfax, while the defence interpreted the same statement as being a command to hand over the weapon to the police. Although Derek Bentley was not the last male to be executed in Britain, the perception that he was executed without having had the benefit of a sufficiently fair trial, strongly influenced one of the most hotly debated and culturally contentious political decisions in British history – the abolition of the death penalty for murder in 1965 (and, as a result of these misgivings and inconsistencies, Derek Bentley was posthumously pardoned of his death sentence in 1993 and his conviction for murder was overturned by The Court of Appeal in 1998).

Debate about reintroducing capital punishment remains extremely contentious to this day, and, culturally speaking, attitudes to the reintroduction of hanging are still (to invoke a string of metaphors from visual culture) an almost stereotypical litmus-test [15] of what "side" members of the public choose to take with regard to their attitudes to the conflict between liberal humanist morality and (what's often perceived to be) more "traditional" and authoritarian cultural values. In that context it is interesting to note that such an important controversy was so strongly influenced by a case of alleged mishearing; and it is consistent with another metaphor derived from visual culture – namely the central metaphor explored by this book – that in this sense both the defence and prosecution perceived Derek Bentley's alleged words in a manner similar to how psychiatric clients are asked to look at Rorschach ink-blots tests, perceiving what their own mind-sets predisposed them to (so-to-speak) want to hear. In terms of visual culture, albeit in a fictional context, a related narrative played out around interpretations of the phrase "he'd kill us if he got the chance", recorded by the fictitious audio surveillance expert Harry Caul in the extraordinary movie *The Conversation*, directed by Francis Coppola with sound design by Walter Murch [16]. As usual however, with the Craig and Bentley case, reality proved somewhat stranger than subsequent fiction.

If the extent to which extrapolating ideas about the perception of language from an assessment of evidence as anecdotal as that which arose from a warehouse robbery may seem open to question however, it's worth remembering that the famous linguist Benjamin Lee Whorf extrapolated much of the theory of "linguistic relativity" (the belief that structures of language strongly influence structures of thought itself) from reports of observations of warehouse fires, which Whorf had recorded during his work as an inspector for the Hartford Fire Insurance Company [17]. This theory – the Sapir-Whorf hypothesis – jointly named after Whorf and his colleague the anthropologist Edward Sapir, is widely regarded as one of the most important concepts in 20th century linguistics (and Benjamin Lee Whorf is also famous for his pioneering studies of Native American languages and of Mayan and Aztec hieroglyphs).

With regard to the subject of visual illusions, the ambiguous testimony presented in the Craig and Bentley case in particular suggests a close (although again anecdotal) aural analogue of the illusory rhomboid published by the Swiss crystallographer Louis Albert Necker in 1832 [18][19]. As described by the evolutionary biologist Richard Dawkins in his book *The Extended Phenotype*, the Necker Cube is a line-drawing that "the brain interprets as a three-dimensional cube", where "there are two possible orientations of the perceived cube", both of which are "equally compatible with the two-dimensional image on the paper" [20]. Any corner of a Necker Cube line-drawing can be interpreted as being on a face of the cube that is closest to the viewer in three-dimensional space, while the same face can just as easily be interpreted as being that which is the furthest away, entirely depending on how viewers happen to interpret that image (so the nature of the comparison with interpretations of the phrase "Let him have it" is hopefully self-evident). Richard Dawkins says that "we usually begin by seeing one of the two orientations, but if we look for several seconds the cube flips over in the mind, and we see the other apparent orientation... after a few more seconds the mental image flips back and it continues to alternate as long as we look at the picture", concluding that "the point is that neither of the two perceptions of the cube is the correct or true one" as they are both "equally correct"; and it is worth stressing here, as with Derek Bentley's alleged instruction to Chris Craig, that these alternate interpretations are not just ambiguous, but in fact they totally contradict each other.

Dawkins does not discuss Necker Cube illusions as mere forms of visual novelty however, but, with regard to theories of evolutionary biology, he regards their ambiguity as a visual metaphor to demonstrate (with regard to his own writing) "that it is possible for a theoretical book to be worth reading even if it does not advance testable hypotheses, but seeks, instead, to change the way we *see*" (emphasis added). In fact I do not think it would be too presumptuous to add here that what Dawkins really means by the word "see" is in this context that he wishes to change the way that people *think*. The specific shift in perspective that Richard Dawkins advocates is one in which humans switch from viewing biology as a study of "whole organisms" and "individual bodies", as they appear to us from the point-of-view of our own visual nervous systems, to an interpretation of biology as "seen" (so-to-speak) from the point-of-view of DNA itself. The alternate perspective that Dawkins advocates is a view in which the "genetic fragments" of DNA "play out their tournaments of manipulative skill" and "manipulate the world and shape it to assist their replication... by moulding matter into large multicellular chunks which we call organisms". So, the implication of Dawkins' argument is that the impact of such reversals in perspective on human understanding may be truly profound, even if and when the illustrations that have been used to explain them are essentially anecdotal.

Subject to being proven wrong by people who know more about mathematics than I do, it is tempting to speculate that a further analogy here may be with the solution of quadratic equations, in which (I believe) a single specific, discrete and formally-defined problem, produces not one but two equally correct solutions. By extension, on a common-sense level, I am sure we all know of situations in which groups or individuals furiously debate opposing sides of a bitterly contested political or ethical problem, about which we are encouraged to take sides with regard to their opposing views, despite the fact that their superficially conflicting beliefs about the relevant subject are both (despite appearances) simultaneously true. In formal research it may also be the case that investigators may, sometimes for professional as well as for purely scientific reasons, develop what the Cambridge pathologist Ian Beveridge referred to as "parental affection" for theories and for hypotheses [21], when superficially rival hypotheses may likewise be simultaneously accurate descriptions of (for instance) different aspects of the same phenomenon (in fact Ian Beveridge warns against developing parental affection for false rather than for competing hypotheses, but his point about parental affection is still relevant in both contexts nonetheless).

In the context of visual culture, the ambiguity expressed by the Necker Cube illusion is parodied in the form of an impossible object held by a young man depicted at the bottom of the great artist MC Escher's lithograph *Belvedere*, illustrated in 1958 [22]. This ambiguity is also mirrored in *The Analysis of Beauty* – an installation created by the author of this book in late 1999, which is exhibited under the authorship of the art project Disinformation. *The Analysis of Beauty* is an optokinetic installation whose title is taken from the book of the same name that was self-published by the British artist William Hogarth in 1753, and a video of the Disinformation exhibit is available to watch on YouTube [23]. In his original book William Hogarth propounded an entire aesthetic theory, developed around the intrinsic beauty of sinusoidal, "S"-shaped, wavy shapes and forms, which Hogarth referred to as those forms which expressed the "Serpentine Line", and it is this aesthetic theory which became the conceptual cornerstone of what Hogarth called his "War with the Connoisseurs" [24].

In a manner very similar to the experiment with ultrasonic visual music described by JG Ballard in his classic science-fiction story *The Sound Sweep* [25], *The Analysis of Beauty* exhibit uses outputs from minutely-tuned audio sine-wave generators to create a slowly rotating, luminous green triple-helix on the screen of a laboratory oscilloscope, with that image being composed from smoothly interlacing "Serpentine" lines (and of course this exhibition theme has been repeatedly proposed to, and rejected by, London's Serpentine Gallery). The motion of the triple-helix resembles, for instance, a rotating rope, or vortex of water, seen sideways-on as though flowing along an imaginary tube. The structure of this pattern also strongly, albeit subjectively, resembles the double-helical structure of DNA, with the impression that this image represents something organic being reinforced by the almost photosynthetic luminosity of the green phosphor on the oscilloscope screen. It is appropriate therefore that *The Analysis of Beauty* was first publicly exhibited at Kettle's Yard Gallery in Cambridge alongside one of Francis Crick and James Watson's surviving models of DNA [26] (although, as I understand it, all of Crick and Watson's several DNA models were working hypotheses, subject to continual and on-going modification, so none of their surviving models are "original" in the strictest sense of the word). Indeed, in his catalogue for the *Noise* exhibition at Kettle's Yard, the scientific historian Simon Schaffer quotes the biologist William Bateson (the man who invented the term "genetics") as stating that "a living thing is not matter..." but a "vortex through which matter passes" [27] (and William Bateson was, gardeners take note, the director of the same research institute that developed the famous John Innes brand of compost).

To return to the subject of perceptual ambiguity, the pattern produced on the oscilloscope as used in *The Analysis of Beauty* exhibit creates an optical illusion known as the Kinetic Depth Effect, which was described by the psychologists Hans Wallach and DN O'Connell in 1953 [28]. The Kinetic Depth Effect occurs when the motion of two-dimensionally flat visual shapes produces (in this case quite distinct) perceptions of three-dimensional form, despite the absence of *any* of the object precedence, motion parallax, aerial and geometric perspective, and stereoscopic depth cues that are traditionally believed to enable people to perceive three-dimensional visual space. The term object precedence refers to depth information that is perceived as a result of close objects partially obscuring other objects that are further away; the term motion parallax refers to depth that we perceive as a result of our understanding of how such objects are likely to move relative to each other, as viewers themselves move through the visual field; the term aerial perspective refers to objects in the far distance growing fainter as they're increasingly obscured by atmospheric mist or haze; the word geometric refers to linear or vanishing-point perspective – objects becoming smaller in the distance; and stereoscopic depth cues are those which provide spatial information as a result of the mind comparing images that it receives through binocular vision, through two eyes (in other words the kind of depth perceptions that it's possible to reproduce using stereoscopic viewing devices, such as the Viewmaster optical toy that was popular throughout much of the 20th century).

Wallach and O'Connell originally conjured Kinetic Depth Effects using shadows of solid objects and of wire-frame constructions, which they back-projected using point light-sources onto a translucent screen. The illusion that fascinated these scientists is referred to as "kinetic" because the back-projected shadows seemed to transform from two-dimensional silhouettes into images of recognisably three-dimensional objects only when these objects began to *rotate* on an unseen platform. It is important to understand that the kinetic aspect of this phenomenon is critical – the impression of visual depth does not manifest if the pattern that produces it is not moving (hence the equivalent effect in viewing *The Analysis of Beauty* installation cannot ever be fully represented by a still photograph).

In addition to this, the rotating form of *The Analysis of Beauty* exhibit also displays vivid perceptual flipping of the exact same type discussed by Richard Dawkins in relation to the Necker Cube and to DNA. The rotation of this installation's triple-helix appears to spontaneously change direction, flipping from left to right and sometimes vice-versa, occasionally flipping for no apparent reason, sometimes changing when viewers momentarily "reset" their vision by blinking or tilting the head, and sometimes flipping because viewers simply *think* about the form they are looking at in a slightly different way. The flipping effect may be reflexive and spontaneous – in that sense unconscious, although, paradoxically, it is still part of consciousness. Alternatively the flipping may be deliberately, wilfully and therefore consciously induced, by a pro-active decision of creative thought. However, as when the mind creates and projects the modified sound "da" onto the visual imagery seen while watching the McGurk Effect videos, the perceptual flipping displayed by *The Analysis of Beauty* exhibit takes places not on the flat screen of the oscilloscope, but inside the minds of those viewers who are watching it.

Kinetic Depth Effect phenomena demonstrate the critical role that not just direct sensations – the raw uninterpreted data that the eyes send straight to the brain – but that *knowledge* also plays in the active formation of visual experiences. Demonstrating such illusions (whether through the medium of scientific demonstration or through the medium of art) allows us to "see" the normally reflexive, unconscious and therefore hidden processes by which the mind, in a manner of speaking, rummages through the collection of shapes and forms which it recorded into memory primarily during childhood play, and by which the mind attempts to match its generalised representations of those memorised shapes that fit best as plausible and viable real-world explanations for the ambiguous sense-data being presented by *The Analysis of Beauty* exhibit, by the Necker Cube, and indeed under normal circumstances by all other visual forms. The same process also enables the mind not just to recognise, but in fact, at a much more fundamental level, to see the objects and spaces that we encounter in the everyday world.

Francis Crick and his colleague Christoph Koch describe the same process, but also suggest that some of the knowledge required for the interpretation and perception of shapes and forms may be stored in and retrieved from DNA itself, as well as being stored in individually-learned memories (memories built-up from, for instance, childhood play with wooden blocks, plastic bricks and other toys, games and interactions with the visual environment etc). Crick and Koch state that "although the main function of the visual system is to perceive objects and events in the world around us, the information available to our eyes is not sufficient by itself to provide the brain with its unique interpretation of the visual world". Because of this "the brain must use past experience (either its own or that of our distant ancestors, which is embedded in our genes) to help interpret the information coming into our eyes", and an example of this "would be the derivation of the three-dimensional representation of the world from the two-dimensional signals falling onto the retinas of our two eyes or even onto one of them". Crick and Koch continue by noting that "visual theorists would also agree that seeing is a *constructive* process, one in which the brain has to carry out complex activities (sometimes called computations) in order to decide which interpretation to adopt of the ambiguous visual input" (emphasis added) [29]. Theorists such as the founder of The Center for Advanced Visual Studies at MIT, the painter György Kepes, describe this process as being not only constructive, but also as being *creative*, by direct analogy with artistic creativity [30].

To return to the imagery produced by the artist William Hogarth, the *Satire on False Perspective* that Hogarth engraved to illustrate John Joshua Kirby's instructional handbook on the drawing of geometric perspective, is a witty play on processes of visual perception that anticipates the work of for instance the Dutch artist MC Escher by nearly 200 years.

The idea that the mind builds up perceived reality, not only from the raw material provided by relatively unprocessed sense-data, but that the mind also employs that same sense-data as references to help locate and retrieve memories and knowledge, which it then combines with the original data to construct and project perceptions that we experience as real, was articulated in the *Treatise on Physiological Optics* by the German physician, physicist, physiologist and psychologist Hermann Helmholtz in 1910 [31]. The experimental psychologist Richard Gregory described Helmholtz's thinking as a theory of "perceptual hypotheses" – a theory that categorises perceptions as "unconscious inductive inferences", which, despite heavy reliance on memory as well as on direct sensation "come about with immutable certainty, lightning speed and without the slightest meditation" [32].

In plain language Hermann Helmholtz was saying that much of what we experience as reality is in fact intelligent guesswork (with the word "hypothesis" in this context being synonymous with the word "guess"). In context of vision, this guesswork is carried out by the mind to help reduce the fantastic complexity of our visual field to a relatively simple array of semantically meaningful and therefore recognisable objects, and to achieve that process of simplification with the incredible speed required to actually make such guesswork practically useful in the everyday world. This last point, about hypothesis-formation being a strategy designed to enable the mind to interpret information quickly, is perhaps best illustrated by the example of reading. A small child first struggles to learn the sounds and shapes of alphabetical letters one-by-one. Then, with progressively increasing fluidity, speed and confidence, children learn to combine those letters into meaningful words, then to assemble those words into sentences, then to assemble those sentences into paragraphs. After this readers may even develop the skill of speed-reading, whereby entire paragraphs, even pages, are skipped-over but nonetheless absorbed insofar as the mind is still able to identify and extract such information as is most relevant to the interests of individual readers. Each stage in this process is characterised by a marked acceleration in the speed of the reading that it enables, and in essence similar processes take place with all other forms of perception.

Edward Nitchie observed very similar skills being used by musicians who sight-read written and printed music scores, when he pointed out that "when you play the piano, the printed notes are your guide, but (if you are truly skillful) these notes are transformed into music through your fingers without stopping to think what the notes are". Nitchie goes on to make a further comparison with learning to become fluent at speaking a foreign language, and then concludes that in both cases "the technical knowledge is there, and is used, but it has been relegated to the lower centres of the brain that do things by habit without requiring attention or direction" [33]. By the time children have grown to achieve perceptual sophistication – from the earliest eye contacts and exchanges and testing of basic and prototypical speech sounds with their parents, through play and through visual, tactile and kinesthetic interaction with toys and objects of increasingly complex shape, texture, weight and colour etc, and through similar interactions with their peers and their environmental space etc – children's minds develop an extraordinarily well-developed capacity to store memories of (for instance) how shapes and sounds behave, and to recruit those memories to help reduce a potentially overwhelmingly complex sensory field down to a navigable array of recognisable and semantically and emotionally meaningful objects. So, as a result, and whether we are explicitly conscious of this fact or not, as we grow older we all learn to "speed read" visual, auditory and other sensory environments, with a skill equivalent to trained musicians performing a musical score. In doing so we become largely oblivious to the process which enabled us to achieve this however, precisely because we have become so skilled at performing such functions so quickly.

The brain is sufficiently well-trained at performing these functions, that situations in which we encounter stimuli that are so ambiguous that we genuinely can't resolve them into perceptually reliable objects are very rare, and it is those mis-perceptions that we experience as (for instance) mishearings and visual illusions. Kinetic

Depth Effect and Necker Cube type illusions represent rare cases of highly unusual visual sense-data, sufficiently refined in their ambiguity that when the imagination attempts to attach meanings to them (meanings which describe, for instance, whether the pattern displayed in *The Analysis of Beauty* installation is rotating to the left or to the right) the brain simply can't make up its mind. In experiencing such perceptual flipping for themselves, viewers feel their own minds trying to resolve perceptual ambiguities in real-time, and in this way demonstrations of such illusions enable and communicate direct and intuitively empirical insights into processes that would be much harder to explain using conventional narrative tools.

If it may seem counterintuitive to suggest that the mind is really capable of imagining, or, even more dramatically, of actually *inventing* aspects of what we perceive as (and rely upon to be) reality, in fact such inventions are among the most fundamental aspects of visual experience, and again we are normally oblivious to vision's imaginary aspects precisely because those inventions are in fact so convincing. A good example of this is that (as is well-known) the visual image transmitted into the eye, through the pupil, appears projected onto the retina at the back of the eye upside-down. This is also the case with images projected onto the insides of photographic cameras and the camera-obscura. In the case of our visual system however, it is the mind alone which re-inverts that upside-down image, so that we perceive our visual world as being the right way up [34]. Such corrected images may therefore be considered in one sense to be forms of illusion, but if so they are illusions which help to create practical and usable perceptions of reality, and the same is true of many other forms of illusion.

It was even suggested by the psychologist George Stratton's near-legendary experiment of 1896, that if goggles fitted with special inverting lenses are used to turn vision upside-down, after an admittedly considerable period of wearing those goggles, the mind inverts the entire visual field again, so that the world is seen normally once more; although there has since been some controversy about Stratton's findings [35][36]. That controversy notwithstanding, either way it is the mind that takes the two different images received by the left and right eyes, and, by a similarly illusory and inventive process, combines them both into what we perceive as a seamlessly blended single image. The irony is that in a sense we see a more accurate representation of raw sense-data, when we are (to coin a phrase) so blind-drunk that the mind loses its ability to fuse these images and instead we see double; and, as we shall see later, these facts were well-known to William Hogarth.

Similarly the portion of the retina that folds back into the rear of the eye to transmit information to the brain along the optic nerve is insensitive to light, and this feature produces a circular blind-spot (also known as a scotoma) reported to be approximately 6.5° wide across the visual field [37]. Were it the case that biology forced humans to navigate our visual world with two dirty great holes in front of us all the time, this obstruction would be a severe impairment, were the mind not constantly (to borrow an analogy from desk-top publishing) copying textures from the visual fields that surround those blind-spots, and from equivalent spaces in the images received by the opposite eyes, and "pasting" those textures over the blind-spots to create illusions of smoothly continuous visual fields. As described by the psychologists Carole Wade and Carol Tavris "we are unaware of the blind spot because... the image projected on the spot is hitting a different, non-blind spot on the other eye... our eyes move so fast that we can pick up the complete image, and... the brain tends to *fill in the gap*" (emphasis added) [38].

In fact the existence of this projective faculty is easy to demonstrate. Simply draw two dots, about 5mm wide and 10cm apart on a card, and then move the card backwards and forwards in front of your eyes. Cover your right eye with your right hand, and, holding the card with your left hand, focus your left eye on the right point, but remain aware of the left dot as it appears in your peripheral vision. Keeping the left eye still focussed on the right point, move the card to and fro, adjusting the viewing distance until the left dot... disappears. The disappearance takes place at the distance where the image of the left dot happens to have fallen (within the eye) onto the blind-spot (and of course the demonstration can be repeated while covering your left eye, and using the right eye to watch the left dot as well, in which case it is the right dot that disappears). As described, the blind-spot experiment is usually conducted using a visual background of clean white paper or card, but works just as well against a background of complex textures. It can, with some care (or bad luck) even be used to make distant people or (much more dangerously) vehicles disappear from the field of view.

From the point of view of this particular discourse however, the aspect of the blind-spot phenomenon that is most interesting here, is not the obvious physiological truism, that the visual system passively fails to perceive a particular point, but first the fact that the mind actively creates images which it uses to fill-in the missing information, and second the fact that we perceive these illusory fill-ins not only as amusing visual novelties and experimental anomalies, but as necessary elements of everyday reality. The ramifications of this last aspect are profound – not so much from the point of view of "proving" that reality (or at least some aspect of reality) is comprised of illusions, but more from the point of view of showing how some illusions have been evolved to help us to construct and to navigate reality accurately.

So, given that, in the ways described above, it is the mind's ability to pro-actively transform and to invent visual experiences that paradoxically allows us to see normally at all, it is less surprising that the mind is also able to invent other aspects of what we perceive as reality. In fact a sophisticated understanding of these faculties was demonstrated as long ago as 1753, when William Hogarth wrote in *The Analysis of Beauty* that "experience teaches us that the eye may be subdued and forced into forming and disposing of objects even quite contrary to what it would naturally see them, by the prejudgment of the *mind*" (emphasis added). In a passage that anticipates the interest shown in such aspects of vision by evolutionary biologists like Richard Dawkins and Francis Crick, Hogarth then stated that "surely this extraordinary perversion of the sight would not have been suffr'd, did it not tend to great and necessary purposes, in rectifying some deficiencies which it would otherwise be subject to"; and, with regard to such "great and necessary purposes", we can only speculate what Hogarth might of said had *The Analysis of Beauty* been written after Charles Darwin's *The Origin of Species*. Finally Hogarth pointed out that "the mind itself may be so imposed upon as to make the eye see falsely as well as truly", citing the evidence that were it not for the control that the mind exercises over vision "we should not only see things double, but upside-down, as they are painted upon the retina, and as each eye has distinct sight" (original spellings) [39].

Demonstrations of visual phenomena like the Kinetic Depth Effect and Necker Cube illusions help illustrate how it is that perceptions are pro-actively, and, in that sense, creatively constructed by the mind, inside the mind, and then projected onto the environment, by an imagination that uses data provided by sense inputs to make intelligent guesses about the same environment that provided that data in the first place. While it may be tempting to dismiss illusions as anomalous experiences of no more significance than that of beguiling tricks, upon considered analysis, important illusions reveal themselves as being created by the same neurological processes which create that which we normally perceive as real.

Although much of what we perceive as real is generated by the same cognitive processes that produce illusions, it should not however be argued that reality is therefore in any way fundamentally illusory, because the projections that the mind generates to help us to understand and make sense of our world are, except in rare cases, for most everyday practical purposes, exceptionally accurate and trustworthy descriptions of reality.

The comparison between perceptual creativity and the field of specifically (even professionally) artistic creativity is further echoed in the quotation from JG Ballard that opens this chapter. Ballard described the central nervous system as projecting images into the mind's eye in a manner equivalent to the artists Michelangelo di Buonarroti and Sandro Botticelli painting the inside of the Sistine Chapel [40], and, from an aesthetic point of view, the implications of such an analogy are hopefully clear. Later on the same page, Ballard goes on to describe consciousness as an "artefact" which allows the nervous system to "make its way around internal and external environments". That Ballard ascribed this (beautiful) process to "nature" itself, rather than to the owner of each individual nervous system, at least implies a reversal of perspective similar to Richard Dawkins' statements about "seeing" evolution from the point-of-view of DNA. Again echoing Richard Dawkins, Ballard understood this process as being firmly rooted in biological imperatives – as resulting from the need for "maintaining ourselves and reproducing our species". However Ballard was wrong to then suggest that "the visual space we occupy doesn't actually coincide with the external world", as in fact, and as I hope this discourse has demonstrated, the perceptions that the brain (so-to-speak) "paints" are (under most circumstances) incredibly sophisticated and reliable representations of reality.

In very similar ways to how Kinetic Depth Effects and Necker Cube illusions enable people to feel the mind trying to "best-fit" viable interpretations onto unusually ambiguous visual representations of shapes and forms, previous *Rorschach Audio* articles have detailed numerous examples of how the mind attempts to best-fit viable meanings to ambiguous, distorted and partially obscured sounds [41]. By way of a brief recap, experiments by psychologists such as Diana Deutsch and Ulric Neisser involved using endlessly repeated recordings of meaningless or semantically-neutral speech fragments, onto which the mind projects a series of constantly evolving, illusory and sometimes quite bizarre interpretations. As described in the earlier *Rorschach Audio* articles, similar experiments have been unwittingly conducted by so-called Electronic Voice Phenomena researchers, who believe that their own (wildly unscientific) experiments reveal "electronic proof" that recordings of misheard radio voices are recordings of ghosts. Equally spurious conclusions have been reached by Christian Evangelist "back-masking" researchers, who propagandise related mishearings as alleged proof of covert Satanic influence in Heavy Metal music (and one paradox of the latter is that, ideologically-speaking, there definitely is Satanist influence in Heavy Metal music, but that influence is entirely man-made and definitely not supernatural). Likewise, descriptions by Leonardo

Da Vinci, EH Gombrich, Indu K Mallah and Geoffrey Grigson, and sound imagery in the vernacular poem *London Bells* ("Oranges and Lemons..."), all document instances of the mind trying to best-fit meaningful speech sounds onto similarly repetitive noises produced by bell-ringing, by rattling trains and by rotating mill-wheels. Perhaps the existence of EVP research within today's technological culture is not so surprising however, as mankind's propensity to anthropomorphise sounds of howling wind, and to imagine those sounds as the cries of wailing ghosts seems so ancient as to be virtually primeval, and because grief will unfortunately never die. All of these illusions, of sound and of vision, are fully consistent with the theory which understands perceptions as "perceptual hypotheses".

Both intuitively, and in context of such a weight of accumulated evidence, it seems frankly bizarre that myths still persist about the alleged passivity attributed to our sense of hearing. As one example, in his (fantastically erudite, but occasionally self-contradictory) book *I See A Voice* (subtitled "Deafness, Language and the Senses – a Philosophical History") the philosopher Jonathan Rée is almost accusatory in attributing "little more than supine passivity" to the sense of hearing [42]. Listening to for instance the ambiguous vocal loops prepared by the psychologist Diana Deutsch for her *High-Low* demonstration [43], the sense of hearing seems to almost interrogate sound, actively demanding listeners' focussed attention, and extracting a tangible effort of imaginative concentration in order to try and resolve the recording's perplexing ambiguity. Although Jonathan Rée goes on to cite medical auscultation (stethoscope use by doctors) as an example of professionally specialised active listening, even then his perspective still seems heavily biased towards disparaging hearing as somehow passive. As a case in point, Rée discusses the "lowliness of hearing compared with the lordliness of vision", and (while there's an obvious risk in taking short quotes out of context as representative of anyone's thought) Rée also quotes the Frankfurt School philosopher and musicologist Theodor Adorno to suggest that hearing is "unconcentrated and passive" and "dozy and inert" [44].

In his own case at least Jonathan Rée makes the origin of his attitude autobiographically clear. He states that "when I was a child, I used to love playing around with my visual world", and describes hours spent "shutting first one eye and then the other, making things move from left to right and back again, or watching distorted people through old fashioned irregular windowpanes", and many similar games, before stating that "there were not many such games to be played with my hearing", as "I had no real control over my ears". Similarly the mathematician and physicist Ivars Peterson quotes the leading sound theorist R Murray Schafer as stating that "The sense of hearing cannot be closed off at will. There are no earlids. When we go to sleep our perception of sound is the last door to be closed and it is also the first to open when we awaken" [45].

The observation that we have no equivalent of eyelids with which to control hearing is a physiological truism that hides a potentially serious misunderstanding however. Just for a start, it is equally obvious that children and adults can and do control their hearing by putting their fingers in and hands over their ears to reduce unwanted sounds, by cupping hands over the ears to focus and amplify faint or distant sounds, and by placing their ears against objects and surfaces to listen for previously hidden sounds. Jonathan Rée states that his ears "could not be closed or swivelled", despite the fact that ears can be closed, and despite no-one needing to swivel ears independently when ears are attached to heads and necks which swivel perfectly well anyway. After this, Rée does then however get cold feet about his initial statement, admitting that "though I *might* block (my ears) with my fingers..." (emphasis added) "I could not shut out external sound completely" (as if the latter was significantly different from vision in that respect, as blocked ears still admit some sound just as closed eyelids still admit some light). Finally he states that "all I could do with my ears was to take them with me to different places, like a pair of buckets, and wait for them to collect whatever sounds happened to drop into them".

If the extent to which we can and do control hearing may sometimes be overlooked for the simple reason that humans don't have muscles in our ears, other mechanisms that we use to control hearing are more complex and subtle. On a reflexive rather than explicitly intentional level, no doubt we've all experienced how some people simply don't hear others talking to them when that person is absorbed in for instance reading a newspaper or a book, my mother reports how the clicks and scratches on old vinyl records seem to disappear after she's been listening to them for a while, and anyone who's lived close to a railway line, to a main road or to an airport knows that after a few days' adaptation to such noisy environments, most of us simply stop hearing those sounds at all (unless our attention is deliberately drawn to them). A related phenomenon manifests on the rare occasions I'm lucky enough to set off on a long-haul flight – I find the sound-ambience in the aircraft deafening after the plane's just taken off, seeming considerably quieter by the time the flight's ready to land after some hours. Although admittedly in context of a novel, EM Forster described a fictional but plausible scenario in which "the Machine hummed eternally" but "she did not notice it, for she had been born with it in her ears" [46]. In such instances we either hear sounds less, or in some cases simply stop hearing certain sounds at all, not because we have chosen to use any physical barrier to control their volume, and not because the mind has in any sense turned down the volume of hearing itself overall, but because the mind has selectively identified and then reduced or even removed certain specific sounds, editing those sounds out of our hearing because the mind is not interested in listening to them.

One utilitarian (in this case medical) advantage to understanding such processes is amply demonstrated by the fact that the operation of a similar faculty is central to the mechanism identified in the audiological neuroscientist Pawel Jastreboff's theory of tinnitus, or ringing ears. Pawel Jastreboff found that experimental test-subjects – ordinary people who were not normally suffering the stressful symptoms of ringing ears, still tend to experience tinnitus after they've been sitting in an anechoic and heavily sound-proofed chamber for some time. The reason for this is that in such unnaturally quiet chambers, the mind, expecting to perceive the level of background noise its grown accustomed to hearing on a daily basis, slowly turns-up the amplification of its own auditory system, as it searches the environment for a reassuringly normal level of natural background noise. As a result of this increasing amplification, test-subjects start to hear their own bodily sounds, such as heart-beat etc, where previously they'd rarely been aware of them. They also start to hear the same high-pitched tones that annoy tinnitus sufferers, tones which Jastreboff argues are residual operating noise, internally-produced by the auditory nervous system. Since we are all born hearing this noise, under normal circumstances, as when living near a railway line, our minds learn to selectively exclude this noise from conscious perception [47].

Jastreboff's theory argues that if some people experience a (usually temporary) ringing in their ears, typically after attending a loud music event, that ringing usually fades quite naturally after a few hours or days. On rare occasions however, tinnitus sufferers may be so afraid that exposure to excessive noise might have damaged their hearing, that (irrespective of whether they have harmed their hearing or not) they over-compensate for that exposure, by immersing themselves in conditions of unnatural and excessive quiet, with the effect that they isolate themselves from the natural background noise that would normally help mask the sound of ringing ears. In the worst cases they may even wear ear-plugs while trying to sleep at night, misguidedly trying to "protect" their hearing but potentially damaging it more, by inadvertently simulating the experience of spending excessive periods of time in a sound-proof chamber. The concern that listeners might have permanently damaged their hearing can cause people to actively listen-out for the ringing that they fear is symptomatic of that damage, thereby over-sensitising themselves to a sensory artefact that they should instead be "reminding" their nervous system it should be choosing to ignore. In other words the accidental effect of this reaction is that listeners may trick themselves into developing medically problematic tinnitus, when in fact their hearing might even be undamaged – and this effect can be distressing, especially when tinnitus interferes with sleep.

So, on this basis, Jastreboff and his colleagues developed a regime of so-called Tinnitus Retraining Therapy, which recommends that tinnitus sufferers should definitely not seek out excessive quiet, but that they should instead search for and create gently noisy environments, in order to help mask and distract attention away from their ringing ears, and in doing so help progressively de-stress the mind. One good way of trying this is by playing very quiet radio static or gentle white noise in the bedroom at night. In fact Jastreboff's diagnostic model, and the role of psychological factors in tinnitus, are both so powerful that Jastreboff (accurately) reports that some sufferers experience an improvement in their condition soon after the true nature of their problem is simply explained to them [48].

Observations about the mind's extraordinary ability to selectively control which sounds are chosen to feature in our perceptions, are also experimentally corroborated by a classic but cruel vivisection procedure, in which Princeton researchers Wever and Bray "startled physiologists with an experiment on a cat in which they demonstrated that by placing electrodes on the auditory nerve they could, with amplification, hear in the next room the sounds falling on the cat's ear", with these sounds being "so exactly reproduced that not only the words but the voice of the speaker could be identified" [49]. Similar results have been reproduced by many researchers, including Hernández-Peón, whose team measured electrical responses produced in cats' auditory nerves when the poor animals were presented with audible clicks. Obviously the process of removing semantically-constructed objects from perception creates experiences that are just as illusory as when the mind imagines previously missing objects, and Hernández-Peón found that (as with human responses to living near railway lines etc) responses to "monotonously repeated clicks die out after several thousand presentations", and found that his cats "gave smaller responses... when their attention was diverted from the sound by the presence of a live mouse". In other words, echoing William Hogarth's statement about vision, Hernández-Peón confirmed that the mammalian brain can reduce or even remove sounds from perception when those sounds become boring or when something more exciting turns up.

Mary Brazier interpreted Hernández-Peón's findings as suggesting that some of the function of the auditory system "might be the modification of central afferent transmission, and that within its influence might lie the neurophysiological mechanism responsible for listening as contrasted with hearing", suggesting as a result that the mind exercises "an editing influence... on sensory inflow" – a view which definitely concurs with Hermann Helmholtz's theories of perception (the word "afferent" refers to the direction of flow of nerve signals, specifically to signals that travel from the environment, via the sense organs, into the brain). So, the mind's ability to sense an entire spectrum of sounds within an overall auditory field, to identify and isolate meaningful "objects" within that spectrum, and in some cases to completely remove the least interesting of those objects, while seamlessly restoring the rest of the remaining sound-field, reveals a mental capacity of extraordinary computational power and analytical subtlety, demonstrating exactly how, in direct contradiction to the "earlids" hypothesis, the mind can and does "close" the ears to certain sounds.

In contrast to the view that seems to hold the sense of hearing as passive and inert, speaking personally I find it hard to imagine that anyone could have reached adulthood without experiencing the rich variety of games that can be played with hearing – without listening for the illusory sound of waves in a seashell, without listening to the "snap, crackle and pop" of Rice Crispies, without using two baked-bean cans connected with string to listen for whispers transmitted by a friend over a long distance, without listening to a friend, to a family member or to a lover's heart-beat, without holding a ticking watch to your ear, without pressing your ear against the chest of a purring cat, without twanging a ruler and sliding it to and fro across the edge of a school desk to listen to the comical sounds it makes, without revelling in the raw thrill of revving an engine or chanting at football, without listening to echoes inside a cave or abandoned building or beside a steep hill or cliff, without listening to babbling voices as they appear when swimming underwater, or without at least having one go at trying to learn a musical instrument or a foreign language, etc.

The importance of sound in childhood play is further evidenced by, for instance, the fact that the UK National Sound Archive's oral history collections contain 140 *audio* recordings of children's games, recorded by Iona Opie [50]. Even a quick glance at Wikipedia reveals the global spread of the listening games known in various languages as Broken Telephone, Gossip, Grapevine, Secret Message, Silent Post, Whisper Down the Lane and Chinese Whispers [51], and images of active listening in popular visual culture include (among many others) cinematic depictions of Native American trackers listening to railway lines for sounds of distant trains and listening to the desert floor for sounds of horses, endless depictions of audio surveillance in police and spy films, and heist movies which show gangsters using stethoscopes to try to crack the combinations of bank vaults and safes. While I'll reiterate that Jonathan Rée's book is extraordinarily erudite, it misrepresents human perception in stating that "auditory mistakes are never more than isolated errors" and that "hearing suffers from no perceptual paradoxes to parallel the optical illusions" [52]. In contrast my conclusion is that his misconceptions seem to reflect a common prejudice that the great scientist Robert Hooke identified as long ago as the 17th century, and it is such perceptual blind-spots that I hope this article may go some way to helping remove...

"Who knows but that as in a watch, we may hear the beating of the balance, the running of the wheels, the striking of the hammers, the grating of the teeth, and multitudes of other noises; who knows, I say, but that it may be possible to discover the motions of the internal parts of bodies, whether animal, vegetable or mineral, by the sound they make. I could proceed further, but methinks I can hardly forbear to blush when I consider how the most part of men will look upon this; but I have this encouragement, not to think all these things utterly impossible, though never so much derided by the generality of men, and never so seemingly mad, foolish and phantastic, that as thinking them impossible cannot much improve my knowledge, so that believing them possible may, perhaps, be an occasion of taking notice such things as another would pass by without regard as useless." – Robert Hooke (1635-1703)

[1] JG Ballard *The Kindness of Women* Grafton, London, 1992, p.200
[2] Philip MacDonald *Warrant for X* 1956 (re-made as the film-noir *23 Paces to Baker Street* directed by Henry Hathaway, 20th Century Fox, 1956)
[3] Sylvia Wright "The Death of Lady Mondegreen" *Harper's* Magazine, November 1954 – mondegreens are known as "soramimi kashi" in Japanese slang
[4] SH Butcher (translator) *The Poetics of Aristotle* Macmillan, London, 1920, pp.70-71
[5] H McGurk & J MacDonald "Hearing Lips and Seeing Voices" *Nature* 264, 1997, pp.746-748
[6] Jens Bernsen "Lydd i Design" Delta Akustik & Vibration / Dansk Design Centre, Copenhagen, 1999, p.93
[7] http://www.youtube.com/watch?v=aFPtc8BVdJk – retrieved 29 August 2011
[8] Quoted in Ruth Campbell, Introduction to *Lipreading – Visible Language* special issue, Rhode Island School of Design, vol.XXII no.1, 1988, p.5
[9] Arab Strap *Elephant Shoe* Go Beat, 1999
[10] Edward Nitchie *Lip-Reading – Principles and Practise* Frederick Stokes and Co., New York, 1912, pp.7, 12 & 13
[11] André-Marie Ampere, quoted in Jacques Ninio *The Science of Illusions* Cornell University Press, 2001, p.83 (originally published in French as *La Science des Illusions* Editions Odile Jacob, Paris, 1998)
[12] David Wright *Deafness – A Personal Account* Stein and Day, New York, 1969, quoted in Oliver Sacks *Seeing Voices* Picador, London, 1991, pp.5-6

[13] David Yallop *To Encourage the Others* WH Allen, London 1971

[14] Peter Medak (director) Neal Purvis & Robert Wade (writers) *Let Him Have It*, 1991

[15] At the risk of stating the obvious, the "stereotype" being a metaphor derived from the printing industry, and the litmus-test being a metaphor derived from colour tests used in halochromic chemistry

[16] Francis Ford Coppola (writer/director) *The Conversation* American Zoetrope / Paramount Pictures, 1974

[17] Carole Wade & Carol Tavris *Psychology* Harper Collins, New York, 1993, pp.302-303, see also http://en.wikipedia.org/wiki/Benjamin_Lee_Whorf

[18] LA Necker "Observations on Some Remarkable Optical Phenomena" *London & Edinburgh Philosophical Magazine & Journal of Science,* vol.1 no.5, 1832, pp.329-337

[19] http://en.wikipedia.org/wiki/Necker_Cube

[20] Richard Dawkins *The Extended Phenotype* Oxford University Press, 1982, pp.1-5

[21] WIB Beveridge *The Art of Scientific Investigation* Heinemann, London, 1950, p.140

[22] http://en.wikipedia.org/wiki/Belvedere_(M._C._Escher) – retrieved 29 August 2011

[23] http://www.youtube.com/watch?v=QMtz9ciE9M0 – uploaded 15 December 2006

[24] William Hogarth *The Analysis of Beauty* edited by Joseph Burke, Oxford University Press, 1955

[25] JG Ballard "The Sound Sweep" *Nova*, 1962

[26] Adam Lowe & Simon Schaffer *Noise* (exhibition catalogue) Kettle's Yard / Wellcome Trust / Cambridge

University Press, 2000; Joe Banks *The Rumble* (exhibition catalogue) The Royal British Society of Sculptors 2001; Richard Humphreys & Joe Banks *The Analysis of Beauty* (exhibition catalogue) Arts Council National Touring Programme, 2003

[27] William Bateson, quoted by Simon Schaffer, op.cit.

[28] Hans Wallach & DN O'Connell "The Kinetic Depth Effect" *Journal of Experimental Psychology*, vol.45 no.4, April 1953, pp.205-217

[29] Francis Crick & Christoph Koch "The Problem of Consciousness" in *The Hidden Mind*, *Scientific American* Special Edition, August 2002, p.11

[30] György Kepes *Language of Vision* Paul Theobald, 1947, quoted in Robert Wenger "Visual Art, Archaeology and Gestalt" *Leonardo*, vol.30 no.1, 1997, pp.35-46

[31] Hermann Helmholtz *Treatise on Physiological Optics* 1910, Optical Society of America (translation), 1922

[32] RL Gregory "Perception as Hypotheses" in *The Oxford Companion to the Mind* Oxford University Press, 1987, pp.608-611, see also the entry on Hermann Helmholtz, pp.308-310

[33] Edward Nitchie, op.cit., p.37

[34] Lester Lefton *Psychology* University of South Carolina / Allyn and Bacon, Needham Heights, 1994, p.82

[35] George Stratton "Some Preliminary Experiments on Vision Without Inversion on the Retinal Image" *Psychological Review*, 1896, pp.611-617

[36] D Linden, U Kallenbach, A Heinnecke, W Singer, R Goebel "The Myth of Upright Vision" *Perception*, vol.28, 1999, pp.469-481

[37] Lester Lefton, op.cit., p.83

[38] Carole Wade & Carol Tavris *Psychology* Harper Collins, New York 1993, pp.162-163

[39] William Hogarth, op.cit., p.119

[40] JG Ballard, op.cit., p.200

[41] Joe Banks *Rorschach Audio* articles, op.cit.

[42] Jonathan Rée "*I See A Voice – Deafness, Language and The Senses – A Philosophical History*" Metropolitan Books, New York, 1999, pp.51-53

[43] Diana Deutsch *Musical Illusions and Paradoxes* Philomel Records CD001, La Jolla, 1995, tracks 5 & 6

[44] Theodore Adorno & Hanns Eisler *Komposition für den Film* Munich, 1969, p.41, quoted in Jonathan Rée, op.cit.

[45] R Murray Schafer *The Tuning of the World* McClennand & Stewart, Toronto, 1997, quoted in *The Jungles of Randomness: Mathematics at the Edge of Certainty* Ivars Peterson, Penguin, London, 1988, p.88

[46] EM Forster *The Machine Stops* Penguin Classics, London, 2011, p.9

[47] PJ Jastreboff "Phantom Auditory Perception (Tinnitus): Mechanisms of Generation and Perception" *Neuroscience Research*, Elsevier, London, 1990, pp.221-254

[48] PJ Jastreboff, WC Gray & SL Gold "Neurophysiological Approach to Tinnitus Patients" *American Journal of Otology* 17, 1996, pp.236-240

[49] Mary Brazier *The Electrical Activity of the Nervous System*, Pitman Medical, London, 1968, pp.151 & 160-161

[50] *Opie Collection of Children's Games and Songs*, 1969 to 1983, digitised as part of Prof Andrew Burn's AHRC funded Beyond Text project *Children's Playground Games*

and Songs in the New Media Age - http://sounds.bl.uk
[51] http://en.wikipedia.org/wiki/Chinese_whispers – retrieved 12/8/11
[52] Jonathan Rée, op.cit., p.46

Acknowledgements

This article is partly based on "Disinformation and The Analysis of Beauty – A Project History", *Slash Seconds* 7, Leeds Metropolitan University, December 2007 (online journal) – thanks to Peter Lewis; and on a text about the blind-spot phenomenon published in *The Starry Rubric Set*, Wysing Arts Centre / An Endless Supply, Cambridge, 2011 – thanks to Gareth Bell-Jones. Special thanks also to Graham Frost for pointing out the relevance of the Craig and Bentley case to *Rorschach Audio*.